The Corporate Infighter's Handbook

to be return
last date

D0552496

THE CORPORATE INFIGHTER'S HANDBOOK

Winning the Office War

William Davis

Illustrations by John Jensen

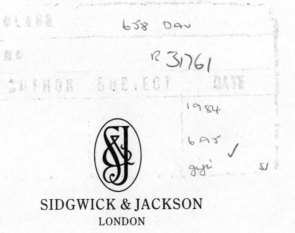
SIDGWICK & JACKSON
LONDON

Author's Acknowledgments

I am deeply grateful to John Jensen for agreeing to illustrate this book and for supplying some of his *Now!* cartoons; to Lawrence Edwards for undertaking the design; and to the Editor of *Punch* for permission to use a number of cartoons which struck me as appropriate.

Other books by William Davis:

Three Years' Hard Labour
Merger Mania
Money Talks
Have Expenses, Will Travel
It's No Sin to be Rich

The Best of Everything (editor)
Money in the 1980's
The Rich: a study of the species
Fantasy: a practical guide to escapism

First published in Great Britain in 1984 by Sidgwick & Jackson Limited
Text copyright © 1984 William Davis
Illustrations copyright © 1984 John Jensen
Cartoons copyright © 1984 John Jensen, copyright © 1984 *Punch*

Design by Lawrence Edwards
ISBN 0-283-99133-X
Typeset by Tellgate Limited, London WC2
Printed in Great Britain by
The Garden City Press Limited
Letchworth, Hertfordshire SG6 1JS
for Sidgwick & Jackson Limited
1 Tavistock Chambers, Bloomsbury Way
London WC1A 2SG

CONTENTS

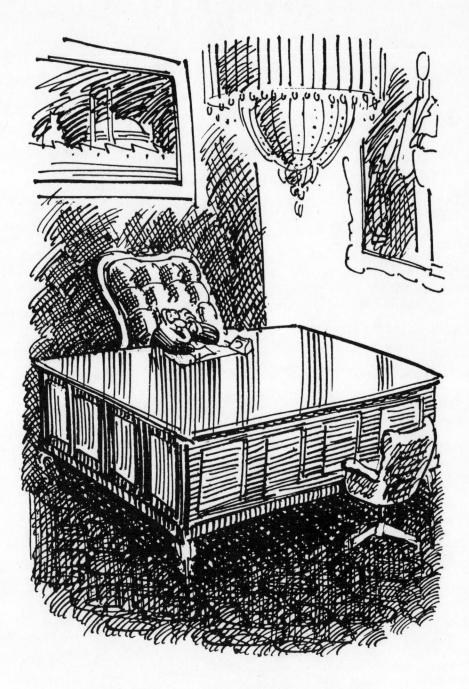

"Mary? Great news! I've been booted upstairs!"

INTRODUCTION

The modern corporation is in many ways very much like the army. There is the same emphasis on conformity, the same obsession with status, the same resentment of 'outsiders' who do not share its aims and priorities. Many corporations have their own brass bands, their own flags, their own songs, slogans, badges and ties. Some even have the corporate equivalent of uniforms: blazers, overalls and the like. Multi-nationals could, I suppose, be compared to a NATO force but they expect – and usually get – a greater degree of personal commitment than an international military organization could ever hope to inspire.

A peace-time army provides fewer opportunities than one engaged in war, so many of the people who at one time would have embarked on a military career nowadays join a corporation instead. It gives them the same sense of belonging, the same reassuring feeling that they are part of a powerful set-up which is bound to last a good deal longer than most of the individuals who insist on doing their own thing.

The stated objective of the corporation is to make a profit. Left-wing activists may regard profit as a dirty word; in the business world, it is a sacred one. Everyone, from the chairman downwards, is expected to acknowledge that it is the reason why corporations exist and why people work for them. The enemy is anyone who stands in the way – rival corporations, trade union leaders, legislators, tax officials – and victory or defeat is measured by the rows of figures in the balance sheet.

From time to time a surprise attack is launched against a hated opponent. It may take the form of a 'price war', designed to grab business away from him, or it may be an outright attempt to take over the entire corporation. The battles

7

are fought with paper money instead of tanks and missiles, but the corporate warriors tend to use much the same language as their military colleagues and are just as determined to win.

Financial writers naturally enjoy these struggles, but don't be fooled by the propaganda. These much-publicized conflicts have little to do with everyday corporate life. *The principal battlefield is the corporation itself.*

Comparatively few executives, judged by what they actually do, are in there to maximize profits. For security, yes. For status and power, yes. For comfort, yes. But not for profit if it means, as it can so easily do, that their personal interests are placed in jeopardy.

A corporation which really made an all-out effort to maximize profits might well decide that it could do so without them. Nearly all companies have more executives than they need, and the most feared person in the corporate world is not the head of a rival company but the new chief executive who arrives in one's own organization with a brief to boost performance by axing the incompetent time-servers, who not only fail to make any measurable contribution to profits, but prevent others from doing so.

Take-over battles may be thrilling for the general staff but they make others distinctly nervous because they invariably produce upheavals. New executives are brought into the corporation and, if they are able, they may move into key positions. Departments are merged, procedures are changed, functions are eliminated. It is a worrying time for people who have grown used to leading a quiet life.

The plain truth is that the vast majority of corporate bureaucrats are primarily concerned with survival and, if possible, advancement. They are willing enough to pay lip-service to the profit motive, but most of their time is devoted to self-serving activities: defending their territory, battling for executive privileges, protecting departmental budgets, recruiting allies, flattering the brass, laying minefields for rivals and getting others to take the blame for their mistakes.

Corporate infighting has never been more vicious than it is today. This is partly because so much of industry is undergoing dramatic changes but also because young executives are in a greater hurry to get to the top. They are, for the most part, well-educated, pragmatic and intensely ambitious, and do not have any great sense of loyalty to the corporation or to their colleagues – though, of course, they are much too smart to admit it. Many of these 'high-fliers' take a job, hold it for four or five years and, if they have not achieved their goal during that time, they join another company.

When times are hard, entire divisions may go into battle against each other. Marketing departments turn on production departments; the finance people turn on both. The public rarely gets to hear about the casualties. Even at Boardroom level, where the infighting is generally more subtle, every effort is made to avoid a fuss. People quietly disappear because it suits neither them nor the corporation to have the dispute advertised. Agreement is usually reached on some face-saving announcement: Mr Smith has gone for 'health reasons' or he has 'decided to retire'. Compensation is often linked to a pledge that the victim doesn't discuss what happened.

As in the army, the most vulnerable executives are those who serve on the front: sales people, production managers and so on. Their effectiveness is comparatively easy to assess. Head office staff who are not directly involved in the business of making and selling things have far more opportunity to disguise their shortcomings. Accountants usually do well because their principal function is to keep an eye on the others and because they rarely take risks. The same is true of lawyers. Marketing experts have also made headway in recent years; the brass tends to be dazzled by their jargon and if anything goes wrong they can, as a rule, get away with blaming the troops.

But having the right kind of professional background is not enough. To survive – and prosper – the executive working for a modern corporation has to learn the art of corporate infighting. It is not something which is taught in business schools and very little is said about it in all those old-fashioned inspirational books which have enjoyed such immense popularity over the years. *The Corporate Infighter's Handbook* is designed to fill the gap.

You may be appalled by the portrait it presents of the modern corporation; surely, you may ask, decent people don't behave like that? You may even protest that your own company is different. If it is, consider yourself fortunate. Alas, ambitious people are not always as decent as one would like them to be: in far too many corporations the kind of behaviour described in this book is all too common. I do not applaud it; indeed, I share the revulsion you may feel. Much of corporate infighting is selfish and cruel. It also wastes an enormous amount

"One of us has got to go, Jenkins!"

of time. I much prefer to work for a small business, where such things are generally felt to be quite unnecessary. My concern has been not only to expose the tactics of the ruthless office warrior but also to show how to defend yourself against them. You will find a good many tongue-in-cheek comments but also, I hope, a great deal of useful advice based on more than thirty years of close observation of the corporate world.

THE GENERAL STAFF

THE CHAIRMAN

The chairman – or, more precisely, chairman of the Board – is the corporate equivalent of the Commander-in-Chief. He may combine the role with that of chief executive but in many cases he is not actively involved in the business at all. There are part-time chairmen who head half a dozen companies and sit on the Boards of four or five others; they flit from one Boardroom to the next and often have only a general idea of what each company *does*. This suits the people who actually run the business because it enables them to operate with the minimum of interference.

At one time, many chairmanships went to retired generals and admirals. Most of them knew nothing about industry and commerce, but it was argued that they understood strategy. The real reason for appointing them was more practical: it was felt that their titles would impress investors, creditors and customers. Some of the companies they were invited to head had been started by people who in World War II had not risen above the rank of lance corporal. These people were rough adventurers who found it useful to have a front man who was likely to command respect. The generals and admirals accepted their offers because, without a war to fight, there was nothing else for them to do.

Today the job is more likely to go to people who have retired from another kind of battlefield: politics. Ex-Ministers are not held in particularly high regard by the business world but they know how to make speeches and understand how civil servants think and work, which makes it easier to get Government grants, defence contracts and planning permission for controversial projects.

Many politicians-turned-chairmen spend a great deal of their time travelling; they are high-level salesmen for the companies which employ them and find it comparatively easy to get appointments with Arab sheiks and Ministers of other countries.

Other part-time chairmen are drawn from the ranks of merchant bankers, insurance companies and pension funds. Their primary task is to act as watchdogs, but occasionally they are brought in to sort out an awful financial mess. They are dangerous because they tend to be ruthless, and the corporate infighter should get on good terms with them as soon as possible.

It is, however, essential to establish where the real power lies. If the chairman is also the chief executive, the position is clear enough. But if the chairman works part-time, any attempt to get close to him may be resented by the people who, in practice, usually determine the course of one's career. Part-time chairmen often manage to push friends and relatives into influential positions, but if a strong chief executive decides to resist such moves he can generally win the day. He may well do so, because no senior manager likes to have the chairman's spies looking over his shoulder all the time.

One of the principal duties of the chairman is to preside over the annual meeting. He has a considerable repertoire of platitudes for these tiresome occasions. 'A difficult year . . . results not unsatisfactory in the circumstances . . . vote of thanks to the loyal staff. . . .' Some are experts at explaining away awkward facts and figures; at one recent meeting the chairman, forced to admit that a major subsidiary had suffered substantial losses, blithely said that it had made 'a negative contribution to profits'.

If real trouble is expected, the chairman may pack the meeting with senior employees who shout down the critics. Or he may hold the meeting in a tiny place, far away from the big cities, which no one has ever heard of and which most shareholders (and financial journalists) have not the slightest desire to visit.

Officially the shareholders are the owners of the corporation and therefore have the ultimate say. In practice, most of them have very little influence. The average small shareholder tends to be viewed with a mixture of paternalism

"J.B. has just had this marvellous brainwave – we'll use your idea!"

and contempt. The only time he or she is taken seriously is when the Board finds itself faced with an unwelcome take-over bid.

The people who really count are the relatively small number of investment managers who look after the huge portfolios of financial institutions. They can, and often do, make changes in the top management and chairmen usually treat them with considerable respect. It pays to get to know some of these characters and to drop their names on suitable occasions.

If you are friendly with an institutional shareholder he can make sure that, when the company runs into trouble, someone else is chosen as the scapegoat. If you can arrange to be his watchdog on the Board you are even more secure – everyone, from the chairman downwards, will be afraid of you and no one will risk accusing you of incompetence or cupidity.

Chairmen are sometimes heard to say that they don't want yes-men. This is a lie: they do. If the Commander-in-Chief wants to win an argument, it is sensible to let him. Your chances of survival – and promotion – are greater if you simply agree with everything he says, even if he is plainly talking nonsense. But it is good strategy, once in a while, to make him wait a few seconds for your 'yes'. Darryl Zanuck once snapped at an over-eager colleague: 'Don't say "yes" until I've finished talking.' Clever flattery is very much part of the art of corporate infighting (see page 58) and there is no excuse for clumsiness.

"So far, sergeant, we've narrowed it down to eight suspects."

THE CHIEF EXECUTIVE

The chief executive, or managing director, is a corporate infighter who has beaten his rivals and is determined to go on doing so. He knows what it takes to get to the top, and he looks on with quiet amusement as others try the same techniques on him. His main concern is to defend the position he has gained after years of effort and, if possible, to add the chairmanship. He rarely has to worry about the intrigues of subordinates, but he is well aware that his Boardroom colleagues will hold him directly responsible for the company's performance. A bad year is usually forgiven; a succession of bad years makes him vulnerable. When things go wrong, he is utterly ruthless: people are discarded without the slightest hesitation as he struggles to escape from his dilemma.

Many chief executives have come up through the ranks; others have been brought in from outside. Some have impressive degrees; others never bothered to go to university or business school. Some are accountants, some lawyers, some marketing experts. Some made it because they have good

connections; some were found by headhunters; some were chosen because they performed well in another company. Most of them are male.

The one factor they are all supposed to have in common is an exceptional talent for leadership. The Board of directors is the War Cabinet; the chief executive is the general who leads the troops. As in the army, though, there are widely different views on how this should be done. There are people who model themselves on Eisenhower and others who try to be a Napoleon, a Patton, or a Montgomery.

The personality – and style – of the chief executive is of such crucial importance to ambitious subordinates that much time and energy is devoted to finding out all about him. The company newspaper invariably portrays him as a managerial superman, but such fawning generalizations are of little help. He is human, like everyone else, and he has strengths and weaknesses which affect the way he behaves. He also tends to have strong prejudices and it obviously pays to know what they are. Let us, therefore, take a brief look at the types most commonly found in day-to-day charge of the larger corporations.

The Team Man:

The Team Man likes to feel that he is in charge of one big happy family; he is fond of platitudes like 'we must all pull together' and tends to promote people who conform rather than daring individualists. A gregarious character, he is a great believer in collective decision-making and holds meetings all day long. He generally acts only if and when some sort of consensus has emerged. Don't upset him by indicating that you find the process tedious, or by airing radical new ideas.

The Computer:

He is the kind of man who judges *everything* by numbers, a human computer who has little interest in personal relationships. His favourite toy, in childhood, was a calculator. He is deceptively mild-mannered; when the figures don't add up to his satisfaction he can be vicious. He dislikes familiarity, feels awkward at company functions and is totally indifferent to domestic considerations. The best way to please him is to keep feeding him with statistics.

The Tyrant:

The Tyrant relishes his authority and rules by fear. He refuses to delegate because he reckons that only he is capable of making the right decisions. Completely insensitive to the feelings of others, he is rude to everyone and constantly reminds his subordinates that he can fire them at any time. His boorish behaviour often hides a deep-rooted feeling of insecurity and, like all bullies, he is afraid of those who are in a position to hand out the same treatment to him. So he generally displays quite a different attitude to the chairman and his Boardroom colleagues. They, of course, are aware of his two-faced approach and tolerate it only as long as his methods continue to produce results. Sometimes it pays to stand up to him: you may win his respect. But it is a risky business – it is much more likely that he will explode and sack you there and then. He tends to promote executives who agree with everything he says. If you find that hard to stomach, leave. All the good people usually do.

The Empire-Builder:

The Empire-Builder is the Napoleon of the corporate world: not content with ruling one large organization, he is constantly trying to acquire others. Much of his time is devoted to plotting the next move. He loves to unleash sudden attacks on unsuspecting victims and he revels in combat.

The press, of course, finds him exciting and he is seldom out of the headlines. But his costly victories often produce more problems than benefits: the newly acquired company may be in a field he knows nothing about (which can be disastrous) or the 'economies of scale' he talked about so grandly when he embarked on his latest venture may turn out to be illusory. Aggressive bidding often produces mergers which are structurally all wrong and it may take years to sort out the resulting mess.

He can, nevertheless, be a good man to work for. He likes to put his own people in charge of the

"I used to be a financial wizard. Once I made an empire disappear."

companies he has acquired, so there is a good chances of swift promotion. Like Napoleon, he creates a lot of new kings and princes. Convince him that you are the kind of person who knows how to run a business, and who enjoys tackling problems, and you may become a chief executive yourself.

THE FINANCE DIRECTOR

The finance director deals in facts, not opinions, and generally commands considerable respect. He tends to be impervious to flattery and charm, and can be a formidable opponent if he thinks you are inclined to be reckless. He expects everyone to do his homework and takes a dim view of anything which appears to contain a sizeable element of wishful thinking.

Many finance directors are dull, unimaginative characters obsessively concerned with detail. If the chief executive is a similar kind of person, the result is usually a sterile atmosphere and little growth. But there are others who pride themselves on their creative talent: they are masters in the art of fund-raising, enjoy juggling with balance sheets and have an impressive flair for minimizing the company's tax liability. Such people are, not surprisingly, much in demand and often make it to the very top.

The finance director's senior aides generally wield substantial power (especially when times are bad) and there is much to be said for working in his department. Those who have to deal with them would be well advised to bear in mind some basic guidelines.

Obey the rules: Nothing is more likely to infuriate financial controllers than a casual attitude to their systems.

Prepare realistic budgets and try to stick to them: If you can't, be sure to have convincing reasons.

Be cost-conscious or at least make every effort to show that you are.

Quantify your arguments: Financial people are not impressed by good ideas unless they are backed by figures. Don't be vague: try to be as specific as you can.

Don't make over-optimistic forecasts: If you can't deliver, you will be in trouble. It is far safer to err on the side of caution and to be praised for doing better than expected.

Don't try to bluff your way out of a tricky situation: You are bound to be found out.

"Dull, unimaginative characters obsessively concerned with detail."

THE MARKETING DIRECTOR

One of the most interesting developments in the past decade or so has been the growing influence of marketing people. In many corporations the marketing director now has a higher place in the hierarchy than the once dominant production director. Yet few executives could tell you what marketing really is; even those who claimed to be experts tend to come up with half a dozen different definitions.

Basically, marketing turns the old business concept on its head. Business activity is traditionally viewed as a continuous endeavour to pull in enough sales to keep plants economically utilized. The marketing approach is to take the consumer as the starting point, not the company's productive capacity. You find out what the consumer wants, and is likely to want in future, and relate your current and future productive capacity to those needs.

This allows the marketing director to argue that *everything* should be subservient to marketing – production, sales, market research, advertising – and that he must take a personal interest in every aspect of the company's affairs. To make sure that others don't get in on the act, he tries to make it all sound as complex and mysterious as possible. The idea is to give the impression that marketing is a science – which is debatable, to say the least.

Like economists, marketing people have developed their own convoluted jargon and rarely miss an opportunity to dazzle their colleagues with it. They talk knowledgeably about consumer satisfactions, operational research, concept testing, media planning, soft and hard data, brand strategies and socio-economic planning. It all seems very sophisticated, and since (a) no one can really dispute that the needs of the customer are important and (b) corporations like the outside world to think that they are progressive, the marketing director can generally count on a receptive audience.

He, of course, knows that most of his theories are full of holes and that there is no guarantee that his methods will produce the desired results. Decisions which used to be taken on the basis of experience and intelligent guesswork are now preceded by costly research and tomes of statistics, but they are just as likely to be right or wrong – depending on the personal inclinations of the person assessing the statistics. A classical example is the Edsel: the Ford Motor Company spent a fortune on market studies prior to launching that disastrous model.

Production managers, not surprisingly, resent the power of marketing people. So do sales managers, who tend to feel that they know a great deal more about the consumer's requirements than alleged experts who, all too often, have never actually met the company's customers. It may well be that the whiz-kids, with their slide rules and fancy schemes, will eventually be put in

"As I see it, gentlemen, our next step is to find a market for
Design No. 2."

their place. But it is always risky to challenge fashionable concepts; you may be written off as a hopeless reactionary if you do. It is more sensible to concede that marketing plays a crucial role, learn the language, accept (and even ask for) appropriate market research and *then* do what you have always done – back your own judgement.

THE PRODUCTION DIRECTOR

The production director of a large manufacturing company gets on with the job instead of merely talking about it. This, inevitably, means that he collects more kicks than praise. Everyone seems determined to give him a hard time: the chief executive, the financial controllers, the sales and marketing departments, the self-important leaders of trade unions, even the people who supply his raw materials and components. So he is often the most harassed member of the general staff. He has little time for office politics (and, in any case, tends to despise them), which probably explains why few production directors are promoted to chief executive.

When he is not busy dealing with complaints, or trying to make sense out of the marketing people's fanciful ideas, or coping with bloody-minded trade union officials, or shouting at inefficient suppliers, the production director can usually be found at his desk deeply immersed in paperwork. At Board meetings he is forever insisting that the corporation should invest more money in new, up-to-date (and expensive) plant and machinery. He vigorously protests against attitudes which he regards as short-sighted; his colleagues usually retaliate by blaming him for everything that goes wrong. If old and inadequate equipment leads to delays and breakdowns, it is always his fault. Ditto if Boardroom decisions on, say, wages and salaries result in a strike (though many companies nowadays have a separate industrial relations director) or if a newly-launched product fails to make the hoped-for impact.

The production director may have a science or engineering degree, but he prides himself on being a down-to-earth character. He has little patience with schemes which he considers to be woolly and impractical, and he makes no effort to disguise his contempt for people who, as he sees it, 'have their heads in the clouds'. This makes him a risky patron: you may be tempted to adopt the same no-nonsense approach. Stay away from him if you can; if you do get drawn into his orbit try to be sympathetic and understanding, and resist the urge to air your pet theories.

THE
BATTLEGROUND

THE CORPORATE HQ

The corporate head office is the centre of power, the place where the key decisions are made and where the fate of careers is settled. It is, therefore, essential to secure a foothold somewhere in the building.

Running a division or a subsidiary in another part of the country (or overseas) may be more fun and is generally much more productive. But the corporate head office – known in some companies as 'The Kremlin' and in others as 'The Bunker' – is the main battlefield and one simply has to *be* there if one wants to get to the top of the hierarchy. This is why so many line managers gladly exchange their jobs for relatively junior positions which will bring them into regular contact with the general staff – and why so many head office people dread the prospect of being sent away for a year or two. The corporate HQ is the infighter's natural habitat; the factory, or any other place where the actual work is done, is widely regarded as the corporate equivalent of Siberia. The executive who is forced to work elsewhere for a year or two not only tends to be forgotten but is also more likely to be held to account if things go wrong: he is always at the mercy of armchair warriors who have the ear of the chief executive.

Visitors from head office are universally disliked because of their capacity for making trouble. In companies like ITT they are known as 'seagulls' because, as one long-suffering manager explains, 'they fly in, make a loud noise, eat your food, shit on everybody and fly out again'. But they also command grudging respect because their views tend to carry considerable weight. So they are generally handled with care, even if they are obnoxious and incompetent.

Corporate head offices tend to be large glass-and-concrete edifices, designed primarily to impress. Most of them have little aesthetic value, but in recent years many corporations have started to display works of art.

David Rockefeller, who pioneered this move when he was chairman of the Chase Manhattan Bank, maintains that 'art can provide a company with extensive publicity and advertising, a brighter public reputation and an improved corporate image. It can build better customer relations, a readier acceptance of company products and a superior appraisal of their quality'. Some of his colleagues thought this was a lot of nonsense – 'David,' they said, 'just happens to like art' – but no one felt inclined, at the time, to argue with the boss. Rockefeller went out and bought hundreds of contemporary paintings, plus several cartloads of sculpture. Standard Oil of Chicago did the same; so did Price Waterhouse, whose chairman was quoted as saying: 'It's a fun thing to have, and I feel it has made a very important contribution to the firm.'

One doubts if Michelangelo – or, for that matter, Picasso and Van Gogh – ever thought of their masterpieces as 'fun things', but they would have liked the prices which these Medicis of the modern art world have been paying. Living artists may like to note that the preferred size seems to be about five square metres. It doesn't matter if there is nothing on the canvas except a little black dot in the left-hand corner: the important thing is that the canvas itself should be large. Corporations, after all, have a lot of walls to cover.

Some head offices also feature amenities like indoor squash courts, and in Japan some organizations go for decidedly odd experiments in industrial psychiatry. One uses curved fairground mirrors which allow executives with inferiority complexes to look like giants and cut the arrogant ones down to size. Another has the president's face painted on punchbags and invites employees to release their feelings of frustration. But innovations like these are still the exception rather than the rule: in general, corporations prefer to err on the side of orthodoxy. Executives proudly draw attention to computers and other fancy gadgets – there is much talk these days about 'the electronic office' – but they tend to avoid anything which might be regarded as frivolous.

The principal status symbol is, of course, the space allocated to each executive. Many people hate the open-plan arrangement favoured by some corporations, because it restricts their scope for showing off. It also gives them the uncomfortable feeling that the bosses insist on such arrangements only because it makes it easier for them to keep an eye on every employee.

The late Lord Beaverbrook was a great believer in open floor offices and his instructions were obeyed for a number of years. But then he stopped visiting the Express building – he preferred to work from one of his homes in various parts of the world – and executives quickly went into action. Dozens of private offices were created by the use of partitions, which not only provided them with the status symbols they craved but had two additional merits: they could be dismantled overnight if his Lordship should ever decide to come to the office again, and it was a relatively simple matter to punish anyone who misbehaved by moving the partitions so that his space was suddenly, and dramatically, reduced. Sometimes the office would vanish altogether – the ultimate form of punishment for disgraced colleagues. No doubt this simple and practical system is still being used by other corporate bureaucracies.

An even more common practice, though, is to draw a clear distinction between the various ranks by the allocation of different floors to each level of the hierarchy. In general, the most senior people occupy the top floors and it is

"This is the wall, Foster. We'd like you to knock up some sort of apt and symbolic mural – you know the sort of thing – The Chairman and Board presiding over the Twin Spirits of Art and Industry as they rise from the Waters of Diligence to reap the rich harvest of Prosperity while the Three Muses, Faith, Hope and Charity flanked by Enterprise and Initiative, bless the Corporation and encourage the shareholders."

every corporate infighter's ambition to rise to the floor above. The upper parts are usually distinguished by more lavish furnishings; in some cases, they are also painted in different colours. The directors frequently have their own private elevator so that they can be whisked to the top without having to endure the tedium of stopping on lesser floors and having to say 'good morning' to lowly subordinates.

One of the most humiliating features for many executives is the requirement, increasingly common in a security-conscious age, to show passes as one enters the building. It clearly indicates to everyone that you are of no consequence. People who really matter are instantly recognized and, more often than not, greeted by name. The greatest accolade is to be saluted by the security guards as you make your way through the multitude. An obvious ploy, used by some infighters, is to make friends with the guards and receptionists at an early opportunity (ask after the health of their families, buy them the occasional drink) so that they will remember you next time you come through the door. Others will naturally be envious, but they will also be impressed.

The principal function of head office staff is to attend meetings (see page 28) and a number of conference rooms are provided for that purpose. But they don't count for nearly as much as the other two important status symbols – the executive toilets and the executive dining room.

The executive toilet:

Having to share a toilet with clerks and secretaries is almost as annoying to the corporate infighter as having to show a pass when he comes to work. It may be democratic, but he is not interested in that kind of democracy. A key to the executive loo is, therefore, regarded as a major perk, a public acknowledgment of his status. Ideally, he would like to have his *own* toilet, complete with shower or bath, but he accepts that he is unlikely to get it until he is made chief executive or elected to the Board. It is something to aim for, one of the eventual rewards which makes the whole struggle worthwhile.

An executive toilet must have real towels, not ones made of paper, and there must be real bars of soap. It should also be free from slogans. There should be an ample supply of Kleenex tissues and lavender air freshners. The top man's loo may also have copies of *Fortune* and *Business Week*.

Most corporations have not yet got around to installing separate facilities for female executives (which is sometimes given as the main reason for not promoting women to senior posts) and the ambitious female infighter would be well advised not to make a fuss about it. She risks being branded as a troublemaker.

The executive dining room:

Head offices usually have at least one executive dining room and the right to use it is greatly valued. The official justification for its existence is that it saves time and money – executives don't have to go out for expensive lunches – and that it prevents the unintentional leaking of company secrets. Unofficially, it is an integral part of the elitism which is built into the management structure.

Many corporations have three or four dining rooms, one for each executive level. The most important is, of course, the directors' dining room and an invitation to lunch there is a mark of high favour. This is where the brass entertain visiting tycoons and other guests who could be useful to the company and it is usually located in the penthouse or other regions of the corporate HQ. The food is the best in the house and there is generally an ample supply of expensive wine and brandy, even though the corporation may have strict rules against the serving of intoxicating beverages on its premises. The dining room for top-level executives has tables accommodating two or four for cosy interdepartmental chats, and tables for six, eight or twelve for the larger get-togethers. The emphasis is on low-key elegance. Other executive dining rooms may have a buffet-style service.

If you are granted the privilege of joining these salubrious conclaves, remember a few basic rules. Never raise your voice; do not advertise your greed by piling great quantities of food on your plate; and if there is booze available, drink in moderation. Others will be watching you, and any transgression is likely to hamper your progress.

Car park:

Outside the corporate headquarters, the most useful perk is access to the management car park. Here, too, bureaucracy prevails and protocol is preserved. Lower-echelon executives are expected to park where they can; the top men have their own assigned spaces, indicating name and rank. The chief executive's space is closest to the main entrance door but, of course, he seldom drives himself. It is the chauffeur who has the exclusive right to leave the car in this privileged spot while he waits for the great man.

A good corporate infighter *never* uses someone else's assigned space, no matter how hard-pressed he may be. He knows that if he does so he will incur the lasting enmity of the influential executive who considers it to be very much his own.

THE BUSINESS MEETING

Much of corporate life revolves around the meeting. Executives increasingly find themselves forced to do their jobs in frantic spurts between meetings – breakfast meetings, sales meetings, committee meetings, Board meetings, lunch meetings, association meetings, dinner meetings and meetings to plan other meetings. Thousands of firms make a handsome living organizing them – meetings have become an *industry* – and one American university now has a degree course in meeting planning.

There are obvious advantages in group think: one can exchange information and ideas, resolve problems and conflicts, and create unity of purpose. A command from the top that the executives down the line disagree with may

"Quite frankly, I don't think he's as enthusiastic about these working breakfasts as he used to be."

well be ignored, or carried out in ways guaranteed to demonstrate that it won't work. A group decision has a better chance of being implemented.

But all too many meetings are a waste of valuable time. They are not only hard on those taking part, but also on those who are trying to reach the people who are always meeting. Worse, a meeting is often regarded as an end in itself, rather than as a means to an end. The participants kid themselves that a problem has been solved because it has been discussed and minuted. (Whoever first decided that the record of these long-winded sessions should be called 'minutes' had a real sense of humour.) The executive who has the nerve to ask, a day or two later, what has been done about the problem is likely to get a puzzled response. How dare he come up with such a silly question: 'We've had a meeting!'

The length of most meetings is directly related to the number of people present and, as the numbers mount, the chances of achieving anything decline. There is always someone who hates the idea of returning to his desk. So he takes a molehill and expertly develops it into a mountain. He asks questions, raises points, requests additional data, demurs and delays.

No less irritating is the character who arrives unprepared, picks up an agenda item for the first time and says he just wants to 'make a few observations off the top off my head'. The story is told of a harassed executive who arrived late for a meeting and was ushered into the conference room. He apologized to the chairman, quickly found the point on the agenda which was under discussion, and soon became involved in a heated argument. The meeting was adjourned for lunch and it wasn't until half-way through the main course that he discovered that he had been shown into the wrong meeting.

Often the only people who really ought to be at a meeting are those who send their apologies that they are too busy to attend.

Good meetings don't just happen: they are the result of careful planning, shrewd handling and painstaking follow-through. They may be your kind of meetings: if so, you are lucky. They tend to be the exception rather than the rule.

In America, many companies are or have been hiring outside experts to teach their executives 'meeting skills'. In some cases, the experts actually run internal meetings – the theory being that executives will speak more freely, and more creatively, at meetings chaired by an outsider than at those run by their regular bosses. Other companies have created special in-house units whose express purpose is to make meetings work. Here is some of their advice:

Don't have telephones in the room; outside interference can kill a meeting quicker than an outbreak of bubonic plague.

Don't ask more than five people to attend if the main purpose is to solve a problem.

Prepare an agenda beforehand, resolve the key issue at each point before you move on to the next point, and do not let the meeting wander from topic to topic. Remember Parkinson's second law: if other things remain equal, meeting time will be spent on items to be discussed in inverse ration to their importance.

Summarize frequently. This gives you a chance to repeat and underline important points, and gives the group the feeling that it is achieving something.

Don't rely on words alone. Research shows that an estimated ninety per cent of a message is misinterpreted or forgotten entirely. We retain only ten per cent of what we hear. Adding visual aids to 'verbalization' increases retention to fifty per cent.

There is also a gadget on the US market called a 'consensor' which is in essence a sophisticated computerized vote-taking system. Each participant is given an electronic box about the size of a hand calculator. It has two big dials; the bottom one can be set anywhere from zero to ten and the top one has settings that range from zero to one hundred. You turn the bottom dial to indicate whether you support or oppose the proposal under discussion – zero is strong opposition; ten is strong support. Then you turn the top dial to weight the value of your own opinion – zero means you are not at all knowledgeable about the issue; one hundred means you are an expert. When the participants have set both their dials, the chairman pushes a button on his console which then tabulates the votes, weights them and flashes the group's collective judgement on a large screen. New models include a device which enables the

"Was that your voice trailing behind the others when I said 'Those in favour'?"

chairman to punch in the annual salaries of all those present: every six minutes the rapidly mounting 'cost' of the meeting flashes on the screen.

It sounds great, but the most obvious way of tackling the problem is also the best: don't call a meeting in the first place unless you are convinced that it is absolutely necessary.

Unfortunately, few senior executives have the courage to rebel against the system. Their subordinates feel they have no choice; they dare not risk upsetting the brass by refusing to attend. The next best course, therefore, is to familiarize oneself with the various ways in which a meeting can be turned to one's advantage.

Games people play:

The character who makes observations off the top of his head is easily dealt with; you merely have to expose his ignorance. Others can be more difficult. They tend to view the meeting – *any* meeting – as a battleground.

Here are some of the games they play:

a) The crisis man:
The crisis man is deliberately late; he arrives breathing heavily and carrying a bulky folder. This preserves the image of an overworked executive. He then breaks up whatever discussion has been taking place by mentioning some minor crisis which has nothing whatever to do with the items on the agenda. The aim is to focus the meeting's

31

attention on him and it usually succeeds; the rival who has been doing all the talking until then has to sit there, fuming, while the newcomer acts out his little drama.

b) *The abominable no-man:*
The abominable no-man operates on the principle that the company's interests (and his own) require the instant rejection of every new idea. His reasons are invariably the same:

It hasn't been done before
It can't be done
It's risky

The abominable no-man is dangerous because he knows how to play on the fears and doubts of others and because he has, over the years, developed the knack of making his rivals look foolhardy. He is a survivor, an executive who firmly believes in the maxim that 'if you don't stick your neck out it can't be chopped off'.

There is only one sure way to beat him: let him ramble on and *then* point out that the idea came not from you but from the chairman or chief executive.

c) *The ditherer:*
The ditherer hates to say 'yes' or 'no'; he much prefers to make no decision at all. His usual response to a proposal is to suggest 'further research' or an 'in-depth study' by a working party. By the time the various bodies have presented their reports the moment for action has usually passed.

d) *The spy:*
The spy says nothing; he sits there quietly taking notes and, as soon as the meeting is over, he rushes off to give a biased version of the meeting to his patron.

e) *The company bore:*
The company bore tries to disguise his inadequacy by talking endlessly about the past, telling jokes and spouting platitudes. The others get so tired of hearing his voice that no one asks to hear his opinions on the *real* issues, which is precisely what he wants.

f) *The buckpasser:*
The buckpasser is an expert at getting others to do the work. If there is the slightest risk that a meeting may decide on a course of action he is quick to point out that he, of course, already has far too much to do but that Mr Jones or Mr Smith is ideally qualified to carry out the task. One of his favourite ploys is to saddle rivals with assignments which are virtually certain to end in disaster.

g) *The miser:*
The miser is a close ally of the abominable no-man; his sole contribution consists of wailing about the cost of implementing a proposal. It may save five times as much, or make a lot of money, but he is adamant that the company cannot afford the necessary expenditure. His ambition is to become the finance director and he often wins the argument because no one wants to be regarded as a spendthrift.

h) *The jargoneer:*
The jargoneer prides himself on his ability to make even the simplest task sound immensely

complex. The aim is not only to show how clever he is but also to confuse the issue. The other participants, thoroughly bewildered by his flow of fancy phrases, end up feeling that there must be more to it than they had thought. The most effective counter-ploy is to arrive with some impressive jargon of one's own.

i) The hit man:

The hit man has a 'contract' to destroy an idea or, more likely, someone's reputation. He may be acting on behalf of a group of people who, for one reason or another, are excluded from the meeting or even for the brass. His target may be an elderly executive or a young high-flier whose wings need to be clipped, and he is utterly ruthless. The aim is to make the victim look like a bumbling idiot, so that even his friends will conclude that he is not fit to hold his job. Like the jackal in Frederick Forsyth's famous novel, the hit man makes elaborate preparations. He may, for example, arrange to have the wrong agenda sent to the target: he can then sit back and watch the poor fellow's mounting panic as he struggles to say something useful on a topic for which he is not prepared.

Another tactic is to provoke the victim in such a way that he will lose his temper. Angry people tend to say things which they later regret – by which time, of course, it is too late.

NEEDLE

Games you can play:

You are, of course, entitled to play a few games of your own. There is certainly no excuse for failing to protect yourself against the conference warriors. Here are some basic rules which have been tried and tested in numerous combats:

a) Hold your fire:
Eager young executives often give their views too early and then find it hard to retreat. Wait until you hear what the chairman of the meeting has to say. He may be acting on orders from the brass, or he may be one of those people who already know what they are going to do but who consider it diplomatic to make a show of consulting others. Either way, he will not appreciate an opinion which differs from his own.

b) Never volunteer for anything:
The old army motto is just as valid in the corporate world. Veteran infighters know that volunteers seldom benefit from their efforts. If they succeed, someone else usually takes the credit. If they fail, they get the blame.

c) Keep the minutes:
Keeping the minutes of the meeting may seem like a tedious chore. But it has one great advantage: you can ensure that the record (which may be read by someone higher up) stresses your own contribution and supports your favourite schemes.

d) Recruit allies:
Two voices are better than one:
if you are really determined to get your idea accepted it pays to have allies. Try to recruit them *before* the meeting: there is usually someone who will promise to support you, providing you do the same for him on some future occasion.

e) Laugh it off:
Ridicule is a powerful weapon. If a rival comes up with a really good idea – one which may win him promotion – you can undermine his self-confidence (and raise doubts in the minds of others) by treating it as a joke. Smile and say: 'You are not really serious about this, are you?' If he persists, home in on the weakest aspect of his case (there always is one) and make fun of it. If two or three others join in the laughter his good idea is dead.

f) Use ghosts:
An alternative method is to associate the idea with a once-powerful figure who left the company some years ago and can therefore be attacked with impunity. 'Gerry once came up with the same suggestion' is the kind of comment which will at once persuade all the time-servers that if Gerry (who used to terrify them) thought that the proposal had merit it deserves to be turned down.

g) Never admit a mistake:
Confession may be good for the soul, but it is bad for one's career. Never admit that you were wrong unless you know that your critics can prove it. With luck – and skill – one can usually blame (i) one's subordinates; (ii) the Government; (iii) God.

h) Take the chair:
If you are asked to chair a meeting, accept. The job has two drawbacks: you have to stay awake and you are expected to ensure that there is some sort of conclusion. But there are also distinct advantages. You can control the discussion (or at least attempt to do so) and cut short any criticism aimed at you and your pet schemes. You can allocate tasks and end the meeting when you want to.

Experienced chairmen know that one can often secure agreement on a proposal by using the exhaustion technique. The principle is simple: you allow all the participants to argue until they are utterly exhausted and then repeat the proposal one more time, adding your own views. Most of them will, by now, have lost the will to fight (or be eager to go home) and there is a good chance that they will accept your views, even if they run counter to those they have propounded for the last few hours.

Ten Common Reasons for Holding a Business Meeting

The executives have nothing else to do.

It provides an opportunity to demolish ideas which threaten the status quo.

It gives the impression that something is being done.

People like to hear the sound of their own voices.

The head of the department hates to make decisions on his own.

Enthusiasts can be shown the folly of their ways.

Blame can be shared.

Half a dozen heads are more likely to think up plausible excuses than one.

Rivals can be made to look foolish.

The brass want to see how rising young executives behave in conference combat.

PANIC IN THE BOARDROOM

As in war, there are times when the high command reaches for the panic button. Impulsive thinking replaces calm judgement. The order goes out: backs to the wall and cut costs however badly it hurts. The panic quickly spreads to all departments and everyone slashes away furiously at what he imagines to be unnecessary items of expenditure. Economies which should have been made earlier, and spaced appropriately one by one, are made all at once in a disorderly fashion.

Some chief executives, faced with a sudden drop in profits, lay down targets 'across the board' and refuse to listen to excuses. Ten per cent from all departments. No exceptions. No excuses. It is at dangerous moments like these that the corporate infighter finds out who his friends are and whether his contribution really matters to the company. Every function is on trial and no amount of past success will save those which are judged to be superfluous.

You may feel that it is madness to acquiesce in this headlong retreat. You may be tempted to write a long memo to the boss pointing out that such an orgy of bloodletting jeopardizes the future. You will be right. Cost-cutting should be

"Try mixing some things together, Potts. You've got just three days to save the company!"

a year-round process, continuing and orderly, and done according to plan. Indiscriminate slashing usually ends up doing more harm than good. Sales fall even further; projects which might have secured further growth are abandoned; morale drops to a new low; good people leave along with the bad. Far from getting the company into better shape, the chief executive may have dealt it a blow from which it may not recover for years.

It is, nevertheless, almost always a mistake to make too strong a stand. The boss will be in no mood to listen. He doesn't want to know about the long term: it is *this year* he is worried about. Managers who protest that they cannot make cuts are regarded as people who lack guts. They are not trying and they risk being put on top of his hit list.

Most vulnerable, by long tradition, are the 'non-productive service departments' – advertising, public relations, marketing, training, research and corporate planning. Accountants mistrust them at the best of times, because it is so hard to measure their contribution to profits. When cost-cutting campaigns get under way they are directly in the firing line: they are the people whose efforts are regarded as the least important. Even if they survive, their spending is axed with puritanical fervour. Advertising budgets are cut, sales conferences are banned, telephone bills and expenses are vetted ruthlessly, and carefully planned marketing programmes are chopped without hesitation.

Other departments watch the blitz with undisguised pleasure. They have always envied the life-style of these high-fliers and shared the boss's suspicion that it has all been a waste of the company's hard-earned money. Who needs advertising? Surely a good product will sell itself. Who needs public relations? The chairman can do a much better job than any professional: ask him. Who needs planning? Forget about tomorrow; it's today that counts.

But marketing managers and planners are not the only ones at risk. The purge can – and does – affect every part of the corporation. Who needs training programmes? Can't we cut down on maintenance? Why are we spending so much money on designing new products; what's wrong with the ones we've got? Would we really suffer if we had fewer salesmen?

Let us, therefore, consider what you can do when the general staff gives the order to retreat. Veterans will tell you that the best strategy is to lie low until the panic is over and then to go on as before. But this usually works only if it is a relatively minor campaign. In a major struggle for survival the people who lie low may be the first to be sacrificed. No one is going to miss them. Your chances of getting through the ordeal are likely to be greater if you demonstrate to the boss that you are with him all the way. Say that you agree with his objective and enthusiastically point out areas where savings can be made. Naturally, you will try to ensure that they affect departments other than your own; the aim is to show that you know how to achieve results (which will earn you bonus marks) without getting hurt in the process. The primary target must be *someone else's budget.*

If it seems likely that your department, too, may have to make cuts, try to beat your rivals to the draw. Be the first to tell the boss that you don't really need so many telephones, secretaries and filing cabinets. Make it known that, in your view, the office would function just as well if you used cheaper typing paper and recycled old envelopes. You can always go back to them later on; the important thing, at this critical stage, is to demonstrate that you are the kind of executive who knows how to be tough and appreciates the importance of cutting costs.

Another useful ploy is to invent projects of your own and then make a big show of cancelling them. Announce that 'I intend to reduce costs by 10 per cent, with immediate effect, by not going ahead with the planned market research'. Or 'I shall save 10 per cent by halting work on project X'. It doesn't matter that these projects have existed only in your mind; you are seen to be taking action.

Skilful infighters may actually *gain* from the bloodletting. Superiors who oppose cuts, or who make it plain that they regard such exercises as absurd, may be eliminated along with the telephones and filing cabinets. Executives who have helped to swing the axe stand a good chance of replacing them.

THE INTER-OFFICE MEMO

The memorandum is one of the most useful weapons in the corporate infighter's armoury. Newcomers to the battlefront tend to assume, naively, that the main function of memos is to pass on information and assignments. This, of course, is nonsense. They are written for a wide range of other reasons.

As a substitute for action:

Decision-taking is always a risky business; it is much easier – and safer – to compose a memo. Let us take a typical example. There is a blockage in the company's distribution system; the goods are not moving along as they should. If you do something about it, you may cause a strike or some other unpleasantness for which you will get the blame. So you pass the buck by writing a memo. It takes about a week to travel through the in-trays of a dozen colleagues, all of whom may add comments and queries of their own. By the time it reaches the chief executive someone else – perhaps one of those naive newcomers – is likely to have tackled the problem.

The chief executive will probably write another memo, asking for more details, which then starts its long journey down the chain of command. It is possible, but unlikely, that one of the recipients will take action. If not, it will eventually end up on your desk. You initial it and pass it on to the next man. By that time the problem will either have been solved or be worse than ever. It is not your concern; you have done your job by passing on the memo.

As protection:

Like generals, senior executives sometimes give orders which lead to disaster. They naturally prefer to saddle subordinates with the responsibility, so as a rule the orders are given verbally. This enables them to deny that they said any such thing, or at least to claim that they were misunderstood.

The corporate infighter protects himself by confirming, in a memo, that he is ready to carry out the assignment and requesting approval for his planned course of action. He adds a query or two in the hope that this will force his superior to reply in writing. He keeps a copy of the memo, for use if things go wrong, and as an extra safety measure sends another copy to a colleague 'for information'.

As a tool for self-promotion:

Memos are also used to claim the

credit for successes. The people who actually deserve it may be too shy, or too lazy, to bring their good work to the attention of the men who count. The corporate infighter has no such inhibitions. He is the first to tell his superiors that 'the problem has been solved', leaving them to assume that he is the one who has solved it.

"In your meteoric rise to the top, I suppose you made quite a few enemies?"

If someone in the office has a really good idea the infighter acts at once. While his colleague is still dithering, his memo is already on the way to the top. If the colleague writes a memo of his own he will simply look like a plagiarist.

It is, of course, possible that the brass won't share your view of the merits of the idea. In the event, you will naturally attribute it to your colleague.

As a weapon against rivals:

If a rival makes a mistake, it can easily be brought to the attention of others by a solicitous memo offering help. 'I'm sorry to hear,' you tell your rival, 'that your decision has produced such unfortunate results. Do let me know if I can do anything to get you out of this mess.' A copy sent to the head of the department can do the most gratifying amount of damage.

If the mistake has been made by the head of the department himself you have to tread more warily. He will be understandably furious if he discovers that you have sent your memo to a higher authority. The usual ploy is to mark it 'confidential' or 'silent copy', but there is no guarantee that the contents will not be revealed to him.

THE BOTTLE GAME

Alcohol can be a useful ally; it can also be a dangerous enemy. The office lush is a pathetic figure who sooner or later will lose his job. He may be able to hide his addiction for a time but it is difficult to cover up for long. There are so many tell-tale signs: the boozy face, the shaky hand, the slurred speech, the unsteady walk after lunch. But even moderate drinkers can get into trouble. A small intake of alcohol makes some people extraordinarily belligerent: they say and do things which they bitterly regret afterwards – by which time it is usually too late. Others become ludicrously sentimental. They provide their enemies with valuable ammunition by talking freely about their hopes and fears, criticizing superiors (in the mistaken belief that their views will be shared by the listener), and giving away information which is all too easily used against them. The corporate infighter who cannot handle his liquor is a fool who deserves all that is in store for him.

Veterans know the golden rule: *do your serious drinking at home*. Your wife and children may complain but they are not going to harm your career. Your rivals will, given half a chance.

There will, of course, be occasions when you will be pressed to join in. Business lunches have increasingly become prolonged drinking bouts, especially if they take place outside the office. And there are social events, such as the office party, which you cannot avoid attending without giving offence. You can always say that you are on a diet, or that you have diabetes, but if they won't take 'no' for an answer remember a few basic principles.

Know your limit and stick to it

Ask for something your body is accustomed to; if you normally drink wine you may be able to put away three or four glasses without difficulty, but a double martini may have disastrous effects.

If you are negotiating a deal over lunch, always drink less than your opponent.

Tell the waiter quietly to give you water with a few pieces of ice; water looks just like gin or vodka. If your host is drinking a Bloody Mary order a Virgin Mary – plain tomato juice.

Never drink before an important interview; it may increase your self-confidence but it may also dull your wits.

Never make any firm commitments while under the influence of alcohol: if you think that you have had too much to drink, confine yourself to vague generalizations.

Some people are better at handling booze than others; don't attempt to outdo a journalist, a public relations man or an advertising executive.

If you have to go back to the office afterwards, eat a strong peppermint.

Here are some well-tried methods of ensuring that the more perilous occasions work out to your advantage.

The business lunch:

If you are the host, you will naturally be expected to offer a generous supply of what are euphemistically called 'refreshments'. It is churlish to order Perrier for your guest – or guests – just because *you* have a meeting later on. Encourage others to drink as much as they like: it will make them more amenable. Alcohol helps to oil the wheels of commerce: people tend to be more at ease, more willing to listen, more prepared to agree to some lucrative deal. But keep a clear head: no one will notice, once the conversation is in full swing, that you are having very little yourself.

If you are the guest, it is perfectly all right to ask for mineral water or a Virgin Mary. A glass of wine won't do any harm, but try to prevent the host from re-filling your glass at every possible opportunity. Don't let *him* trick you into getting too convivial.

'One for the road':

If a colleague suggests that you go off to the nearest bar after working hours, to have 'one for the road', tell him that you are driving or that your wife is arranging a dinner party. If he persists, accept. But make sure that he drinks more than you do: let *him* be the one who gets sentimental and indiscreet. Don't give him your views on office politics: he will probably pass them on.

The office party:

There is a stereotype of the office party, much beloved of cartoonists and writers of TV comedy series. It features nubile secretaries who, we are led to believe, spend most of their time evading lecherous executives, and office boys who slap the chairman on the back and, made bold by alcohol, address him as Tom, Dick or Harry.

There undeniably are parties which are just like that – especially at Christmas – but there are many more which are events of quite stupefying gentility. The executive who feels compelled to live up to the cliché image runs a very real risk of destroying all that he has achieved during the rest of the year.

The official reason for office parties is to 'bring people together', to 'foster a sense of identity'. They are supposed to make people feel that they are part of one big family. The reality tends to be very different. Office parties are political events: they present senior management with the opportunity to observe subordinates in an informal setting and they give corporate infighters the chance to (a) ingratiate themselves with anyone who may be in a position to boost their careers and (b) exploit the reckless behaviour of rivals.

Resist the temptation to make the most of all that free booze. Secretaries and office boys may be able to indulge themselves, but *you* cannot afford to do so. Stick to one drink, with plenty of ice and water, and sip cautiously. You'll give the appearance of participating without running the risk of getting inebriated and making an ass of yourself. Try to get close to the brass but don't be a bore; don't tell the chairman or chief executive what you think is wrong with the corporation or talk about your personal problems. *Never* tell a dirty joke. And don't overstay your welcome: leave when the guests are starting to thin out.

THE TELEPHONE

The telephone is such a vitally important tool that it is hard to imagine how anyone ever managed to do any business before Alexander Graham Bell came along with his splendid invention. But, as we all know, it can also be a confounded nuisance. Some executives hate it because it forces them to make instant decisions; it is so much easier to fob someone off with a polite letter. Others resent its constant intrusion on their lives; their idea of bliss is a week on a desert island where no one has ever heard of telephones.

Airlines nowadays have the technical capacity to provide an on-board telephone service, but research has shown that most passengers don't want it. There has been equally strong resistance to screen-telephones which allow people to see each other while they talk. It is so much harder to tell lies when you know that the other person can see the expressions on your face. At the other extreme there are 'telephone freaks' who feel naked if they don't have one close at hand wherever and whenever they may need it – in the car, at the restaurant table and even in the executive toilet. For them, the telephone is like a drug; deprive them of their toy for half an hour and they become hysterical. It wouldn't matter if they didn't insist on sharing their addiction with the rest of us; trying to dodge their persistent calls can be an exasperating business.

Used properly, the telephone can be enormously helpful. It not only saves time but has all kinds of other advantages: comments or promises made in conversation, for example, cannot be used against you in the same way that a letter can. (Some executives, alas, have adopted the despicable practice of recording their telephone calls. They ought to remember what happened to Richard Nixon.)

'Conference calls' enable groups of people in different parts of the country to discuss projects without having to drive or fly to meetings; misunderstandings which could cause serious problems can be cleared up without getting bogged down in a lengthy correspondence; answering services can handle a message without imposing any obligation on you to return the call. The scope is endless. But the telephone can also do a lot of harm, and every corporate infighter should beware of the pitfalls.

One of the biggest has already been mentioned: it is all too easy to be pushed into making snap judgements. Some people are very persuasive and there is rarely enough time to consider all the implications. So, on a busy day, you may find yourself saying 'yes' or 'no' to all kinds of proposals – and wishing, afterwards, that you had not been quite so emphatic.

The caller may have caught you in an euphoric mood, or he may have been unlucky enough to reach you when you were irritable and depressed. It is a chance he takes; the same thing may happen to you when you pick up the telephone to call someone else. The doubts develop afterwards and it is often embarrassing to admit that you have changed your mind. Unless, therefore, you are already familiar with the proposals, and have made up your mind how to respond, it is generally good strategy not to make any firm commitment either way. Tell him or her that you will think about them and either call back when you have been able to give the matter some thought or promise to write in a few days.

Another potentially dangerous aspect is insensitivity to other people's feelings: many careers have been wrecked by bad telephone manners.

Never place a call and then force the other person to hang on to a mute telephone while you finish whatever business you have started in the meantime. The chairman or chief executive might be able to get away with it, if the call is to a subordinate, but it is a habit which is bound to be resented. Some people make two or three calls simultaneously and leave it to the secretary to sort out the resulting muddle. Some even vanish to the executive washroom, so that the poor girl has to make some unconvincing excuse. It is a sure way to make enemies.

Some other basic rules:

Don't be rude to secretaries; it is generally counter-productive (see page 68). A kind word or two will make her feel much more inclined to interrupt her boss, or to remind him to call you back. Rudeness will be countered with indifference or, worse, deliberate obstruction.

Don't say that your call is urgent when it isn't. You may be put through the first time, but after that it will be regarded as a ploy and you may not be able to reach the other person when something is *really* urgent.

Don't claim to be a 'personal friend' if you are nothing of the sort. A good secretary will always check, and if her boss replies 'never heard of him' she will naturally assume that you are a charlatan. He, too, will hold it against you.

Salesmen sometimes use other tricks to reach an elusive prospect. One is to adopt a phoney title: John Smith becomes 'Colonel Smith' or even 'Sir John Smith'. It may impress the secretary, and intrigue her boss, but it invariably produces an angry reaction when they discover that it is a lie.

Don't allow your own secretary to adopt a pompous telephone manner. You may be an important executive, but there is always someone who is more important and who will not appreciate being treated like a clerk.

Don't make impolite or unconvincing excuses for not taking a call. Try to ensure that your secretary – or anyone else in your department – not only knows who counts – and who doesn't – but that she also understands the art of giving plausible and soothing reasons for your failure to respond. 'Too busy' is insulting. 'He's in a meeting' is such a standard ploy that it will automatically be assumed that you don't want to talk, even if you really *are* in a meeting. 'He is out this afternoon' suggests that you are playing golf, which can be awkward if the caller happens to be the chairman or the chief executive.

Don't say you will call back and then forget to do so. It is a convenient short-term defence against unwanted callers, but it shows open contempt for the other person.

Some people go to extraordinary lengths to avoid actual contact. They call back at a time when the other executive is guaranteed to be out – lunchtime, for example. When he returns the call he is told that 'Mr Smith is unavailable'. Mr Smith telephones the next day, again at a time when he knows that the other person is ur..ikely to be there. When the call is returned, Mr Smith is 'in a meeting'. This can go on for a week or more. In the end, the man who started this ridiculous game does what he should have done in the first place: he writes a letter. It may seem a clever way of dodging the issue, but it is also an appalling waste of time. If you don't want to talk to a caller, get your secretary to tell him right away that you prefer him to write.

Don't let your voice betray your irritation if a call interrupts something you were doing or thinking about. Switch on your friendly, cheerful tone – and try to make the conversation as brief as possible. If he drones on, tell him that you have an important overseas call waiting for you on the other line or that you are late for a meeting with your superiors.

Don't slam the receiver in the ear of a caller; it is like slamming the door after a visitor. Hang up gently.

Even if you are not seen when speaking on the telephone, you are nevertheless on parade. Good manners will enhance your reputation; bad manners will help to destroy it.

SURVIVING A MERGER

Take-over bids and mergers can wreck the best-laid plans. You may suddenly find yourself uprooted from a secure and promising spot by a new team of young executives from the other company who couldn't care less about you in their big plans for the 'new company'. Your speciality, your

"I'll say this for Benthorpe – there's a refreshing sort of honesty about him . . . "

responsibility, your talent have come to mean less than the fact that you are not part of the organization that came out on top.

The new men may well decide there is a needless duplication of executive functions and they will generally conclude that their own people are better than those of the acquired company – whether they really are or not. Sometimes whole head offices are eliminated.

This is one situation where people at the top and in the middle are often more vulnerable than the rank and file. If you survive, you will probably find yourself working in a quite different environment. Instead of being able to make your own decisions you will now have to seek permission to do whatever you want from the appropriate department head in the controlling company. You will be bombarded with directives that betray an unfortunate lack of knowledge both of your own company and of its market, and you are liable to be summoned at any time by someone in the new corporate headquarters to discuss 'joint objectives' or 'management orientation' of the two companies. You may come out feeling that your whole world has collapsed and that your best course is to rush off to the nearest executive employment agency.

It pays, though, to make a calm assessment of your position. If you get angry and excited you won't be able to think clearly. Ask yourself, as honestly as you can, what kind of future you may have in the larger group. It may well be that, given the right approach, you can actually secure promotion. Every company needs good executives – indeed, sometimes it is the main reason for a merger. Your task is to convince the new bosses that you are the sort of man who can make a very effective contribution.

Cancel any holiday plans (this is no time to be away from the action) and make a quick but thorough study of their set-up and the personalities of the key executives. Tell them that you *admire* their techniques (even if you don't think much of them) and that you welcome the exciting challenge offered by the new structure. Go out of your way to show that you take a positive view of what has happened. You won't be able to change the course of events, so there is no point in putting up a fight. It is far better to try to make the most of them; the golden rule for executives who are involved in a merger is 'adapt or leave'.

ALLIES

THE 'TREASURE'

Try this quiz:

— What is the name of your chief executive's secretary?
— How long has she been with him?
— Is she a wife/mother substitute – a 'treasure'?
— How much power do you think she has?
— Is she a strong personality?
— Is she susceptible to flattery?
— Does she know you exist?
   If you don't know the answers, you ought to get them as soon as possible. Find out about the others, too, while you are about it. The shrewd corporate infighter recognizes that the secretaries of his superiors can be most useful allies. They tend to have far more influence – even authority – than their humble titles suggest.

The 'treasure' is an intelligent woman, generally single, who has been with her boss for many years. She has been at his side during the arduous climb to whatever position he has managed to secure in the hierarchy and knows him better than anyone else – including, quite often, his wife. She is thoroughly familiar with his opinions, his likes and dislikes, his problems, his moods. Efficient, tactful and discreet, she is loyal to him rather than to the company – if he were to go elsewhere, she would willingly go with him – and she skilfully protects and advances his personal interests. It makes her indispensable, and she knows it.

Some of these paragons may, at one time, have nursed ambitions to become executives in their own right. A few actually make the breakthrough, but most secretaries are content to exercise power through their bosses. It is enough to be his closest associate: to know that he respects her judgement of people and situations, takes her into his confidence, asks her advice and allows her to make a great many day-to-day decisions.

To get on good terms with her you must, above all, show that you are aware of her importance. Never, but never, make the mistake of being patronizing. Nothing is more likely to infuriate her than being treated as part of the office furniture.

> If you have a problem, tell her about it and allow her to offer help. She may be able to solve it, in the boss's name.
>
> If you have a request, give her the chance to pass it on in a form which she knows will produce the desired result.
>
> If you need to see him, let her decide the timing: she not only controls his schedule but is best placed to judge whether he is in a receptive mood.
>
> Be friendly – but not *too* friendly. Don't automatically assume that she will appreciate being called by her first name; she may resent it. Don't attempt to bribe her by sending her flowers (though it is perfectly all right to wish her a 'happy birthday') or inviting her out to lunch. (Her boss will get to hear about it and will naturally suspect your motives.) Don't make improper advances. (As if you would.)

THE PERSONAL ASSISTANT

Many secretaries prefer to be known as 'personal assistants', and if their employer is sufficiently senior he will usually approve – it enhances his own status. (It is obviously important not to overstep the mark. A junior executive who allows his secretary to call herself a PA will be considered arrogant and pretentious.)

It is quite common for a chairman, or a chief executive, to have a male personal assistant *in addition* to a secretary. Such appointments often go to young people who are working their way up the corporate ladder. They tend to be selected for their charm and breeding, and their main function is to run errands for the boss and to act as his watchdog.

The personal assistant is expected to keep his eyes and ears open; he is the company spy with a direct line to the top. The boss knows that his executives will naturally try to present everything in the most favourable light, and he relies on his PA to tell him what is really going on. So the PA spends a great deal of time in the executive dining room, listening to the grapevine gossip, and also makes a point of attending as many meetings as he can.

Like secretaries, personal assistants can be maddeningly self-important: they tend to delude themselves that they are already part of the senior management team. It is tempting to put them in their place, but it pays to humour them. Their greatest asset is their close proximity to the seat of power and they quickly learn how to use it. A PA may see the boss five or six times a day, and he often accompanies him on a business trip, so he has ample opportunity to use his influence. If you wound his self-esteem, he can be a formidable enemy. If you flatter him, he can be a valuable ally.

Never tell a PA anything you would not like others to know. Don't criticize aspects of the company's operations, and the people who are running them, unless you are fairly confident that the boss is likely to agree with you. And don't voice open criticism of your immediate superior, or the way your department is run, even if you have every justification for doing so. The PA will report to his boss, who will probably summon your superior and demand an explanation. Your name may be mentioned as the source of the information, or your superior will take steps to discover who committed this act of disloyalty. Either way you will be in trouble.

Turn the PA's deviousness to your advantage by letting him know how much you admire the man he works for, and how eager you are to implement his decisions. Boost his ego by telling him that he is doing an important job, and win his friendship by acknowledging the legitimacy of his ambitions. He will probably end up giving *you* a lot of useful inside information: who is on the way up and who is going down, what his boss thinks of your department, and what changes he plans to make in the months ahead. He may also decide that his own interests will be served by recommending you for promotion.

THE PUBLIC RELATIONS OFFICER

Public relations is a growth industry: we live in a media age and corporations are understandably keen to create and sustain a favourable image. (So, for that matter, are the armed forces: they all have PR departments.)

The job used to go mainly to ex-journalists who couldn't quite make it in the newspaper world or who were seduced by the prospect of more secure employment. It had a fairly low status. The public relations officer's work consisted chiefly of writing press releases which few people bothered to read and getting free editorial publicity for products. He also used his contacts in the media world to get the boss's picture into the papers, and to minimize the impact of bad news. A great deal of his time was devoted to bribing former colleagues by buying them drinks or expensive lunches.

He still does all of these things, but public relations has come a long way in the past decade. His role is more important than ever before and his status has risen accordingly. In many corporations, he now reports directly to the chairman or chief executive and he is no longer known as a public relations officer: he has been made a vice-president or head of public affairs and he has a sizeable staff to help him. He may even have a seat on the Board. It makes him a man to watch – and to have on your side.

Journalists tend to have mixed feelings about public relations people. They like being wined and dined – and sent on free trips to exotic places – but they are wary of them because they so often have little regard for the truth and because they generally make it more difficult to get at the facts. Newspapermen resent the assumption, so prevalent in large corporations, that the media can be 'controlled'. Effective PR, therefore, requires considerable skill.

The corporate infighter should get closely acquainted with the activities of the PR department, not only because he may learn new tricks but also because it can protect him against the outside world. Few executives are a match for trained reporters and, without such protection, they may be lured into making statements which will get them into trouble with their bosses. It is usually best to let the PR people do the talking – and to let them take the blame if the subsequent story annoys the brass. They can also be helpful in other ways.

You may, for example, be able to secure a flattering write-up in the company newspaper or magazine.

Like personal assistants, PR staff are often able to give early warning of developments which could affect your career. They have legitimate reasons for asking questions – if you did the same, your colleagues might get suspicious – and they tend to be natural gossips. Do what they usually do to others: *use* them.

THE HIGH-FLIER

E very corporation has its high-fliers – those talented, dynamic, hard-working individuals who move through the ranks with enviable ease and seem destined for the Boardroom. Hitching a ride with such people is often a quick way to the top.

The high-flier likes to have disciples who share the high opinion he has of himself. They don't have to be brilliant – indeed, competitive brilliance can be a disadvantage. Their principal function is to praise his ideas and to implement his decisions.

The problem, though, is that these over-achievers tend to be heartily

"I'm aware that I'm capricious and overbearing, Hartnett, but why should you be spared? You should see the way I treat my wife."

disliked. There are always people who are plotting their downfall. If they succeed, their disciples are liable to find themselves toppled at the same time.

Some high-fliers are experts in the art of corporate infighting; they are the ones who are most likely to succeed. Others are supremely confident that they can get there without it. They don't mind making enemies because they are convinced that their superior talents will overcome all obstacles. They are surprised and shocked when they discover that this is not always so.

One of the worst faults of the high-flier is his impatience – his insistence on getting things done *now*, at any price. It may win the approval of the chief executive, but it invariably upsets his more cautious colleagues – especially as it is often accompanied by an open display of contempt for those he regards as 'plodders'. It may also lead him to make wrong decisions and give his enemies a chance to pounce.

Sooner or later the boss will have to decide whether his disruptive influence is really worth it. The answer may be 'yes', but it can just as easily be 'no'. If the boss himself feels threatened by his aggressive drive the answer will almost *certainly* be 'no'.

The disciple must, therefore, be constantly alert to any changes in his patron's fortunes. If he hears that his actions – and behaviour – are beginning to cause disquiet in the higher echelons of management he should start cooling off the relationship as soon as possible.

THE 'HAS-BEEN'

It is always tempting to follow the high-flier's example and regard people who no longer seem to be making progress as 'has-beens' who are of no possible use to the infighter. Tempting but foolish, because their patronage can often be of considerable value, especially in large, conservative organizations.

Many hold senior positions and, although they may have given up hope of further personal advancement, they are well placed to promote the interests of their own disciples. Executives who are only a few years away from retirement can be particularly helpful allies. They have nothing to lose and many get vicarious pleasures out of seeing young people do well. They tend to make very good teachers – they have, after all, spent years playing (or at least observing) the corporate power game.

All they ask, in return, is that you show respect for their experience and status and resist the urge to go after their jobs before they are ready to leave. Don't force them to demonstrate that they still know how to deal with arrogant upstarts.

THE MANAGEMENT CONSULTANT

There is an old gibe that those who can, do; those who can't, become consultants. But that is mild compared to some of the insults levelled at them by their critics. Robert Townsend, for example, said in his *Up The Organisation* that 'they waste time, cost money, demoralise and distract your best people, and don't solve problems. They are the people who borrow your watch to tell you what time it is and then walk off with it.'

Anyone can become a successful consultant, providing he follows one cardinal rule: never actually *do* anything. You can talk indefinitely; give advice and make recommendations; hold meetings and write voluminous reports, but never, never take any action because you are sure to be found out.

Consultants are paid large fees for telling people who are generally older, more important and much more experienced at actually running a business how to do their jobs. In theory, they should be unnecessary. A Board of directors which has to call in outsiders for advice is merely advertising its own weakness, and shareholders ought to draw the obvious conclusion: it's time to replace the people at the top, perhaps by the consultants. In practice, the corporate world continues to make extensive use of them – sometimes as a crutch, sometimes as a shield ('See, we are doing everything we can to put things right'), and frequently because they can be made to take the blame for unpopular measures.

The management consultant's one big plus – as he never ceases to remind those who employ him – is that he is independent: an unbiased expert with a wide, varied background and no axe to grind (other than his fee). He generally works on a one-off basis, so he doesn't have to worry about upsetting anyone – though he invariably stops short of recommending that the Board itself should be fired, even if it is plainly incompetent. (If he were to do so, others would be understandably reluctant to call on his services.)

The independence makes him dangerous at all the lower levels of management and the corporate infighter who finds himself confronted by one of these hatchet men should *under no circumstances* indicate that he shares Townsend's contempt for the breed. Let him waste your time; he will be gone soon enough. Be deferential; he will appreciate it. Don't expose his ignorance; you will not be forgiven if you do so. Be patient when he asks foolish questions; remember that, temporarily, he holds all the cards. Help him by drawing attention to the problem areas (i.e., those controlled by your rivals) and by making suggestions which he can incorporate in his report and pass off as his own.

Many corporations also use another type of consultant – a specialist in a particular field, like marketing or public relations. He tends to be better value than the know-all, because he really *is* an expert and because he can provide an effective back-up service. He generally has a close working relationship with the head of the relevant department and often produces good ideas. It is relatively easy to keep him in line: if he gets troublesome, you merely have to hint that his contract may not be renewed.

Basic Rules of Flattery

Don't be too crass: the other person will feel that it's an insult to his (or her) intelligence. Avoid absurd exaggerations.

Be a good listener: the ability to listen attentively, even when the speaker is talking nonsense, is widely regarded as the greatest form of flattery.

Study the person you want to flatter: comments which may please one man (or woman) may easily irritate another. Discover his likes and dislikes, and endorse them.

Remember the value of indirect flattery: praise expressed through a third party (who can be relied upon to pass it on) is often more pleasing.

Ask questions, even if you already know the answers. Most of us are gratified if others show keen interest in our views. Encourage them to talk about themselves — it is usually their favourite topic.

If you *must* disagree with a superior, always call him 'sir' and start with a friendly remark: 'I am your greatest admirer, but. . . .'

Don't flatter someone in the presence of people who are known to be his enemies — they may become your enemies too. There are times when it pays to remain silent.

Congratulate people who have been promoted, even if you think they didn't deserve the promotion. You may need their help in future.

Teach yourself to remember names. People are always flattered when someone they met only once, perhaps long ago, knows who they are. But make sure you get it right: nothing is worse than to be addressed as 'Mr Smith' when one's name is Jones.

LOOKING
AFTER NUMBER
ONE

YOUR TITLE

All bureaucracies are obsessed with titles; the corporate world is no exception. The larger the company, the greater the range of titles. 'Executive' is no longer considered adequate, now that just about everyone can call himself that, so an extraordinary amount of creative effort is wasted on thinking up more impressive labels.

It is often impossible to tell from a title what a man is doing. Very often he doesn't know himself. His title is not intended to be descriptive; its primary purpose is to indicate that he is someone of consequence.

There are several good reasons why the brass go along with this.

Titles are cheap:

A title costs less than perks like a company car. You only have to pay for a new name plate and a new business card.

Titles are an incentive:

Executives will work long hours, for no extra pay, in the hope of securing a more imposing title. Sometimes it involves genuine promotion, but more often it simply means finding another label for exactly the same job. It is an effective way of making an executive feel that he is making progress, even though he – and everyone else – knows that he is getting nowhere at all.

Titles impress outsiders:

Most people prefer to do business with someone who counts – or appears to count.

A customer who has a complaint doesn't want to be fobbed off with a clerk in the services department; he wants to talk to the chairman. He, of

"This office is one big happy family. After twenty cosseted years, Colin, don't you think it's time you left our protective wing to make your own way in the outside world. . . ?"

visitors while the executives get their work done.

Titles placate defeated rivals:

Executives who have lost the fight but who refuse to leave the corporate battlefield are often given titles which salvage their pride. They may, for example, become Senior Planning Co-ordinators or chairmen of committees which spend months, if not years, preparing reports no one will ever bother to read. They know, of course, that they have been pushed aside. Some eventually join a competitor; some hang on in the hope that the next battle will end in victory for their side; some acknowledge, privately, that they are finished but are grateful that they still have a role, however meaningless, and that the company will go on paying them the same salary until they qualify for a pension.

Titles allow empire building:

Everyone wants his own empire. The chief executive has the whole company to play with; the people immediately below him have to build up their own power base. If they have operational departments with obviously necessary functions, such as production and sales, this is comparatively easy. One acquires staff rather as Napoleon acquired marshalls, with titles like Regional Sales Manager, Deputy Regional Sales Manager, Assistant to the National Sales Director, Deputy to the National Sales Director, Assistant Deputy National Sales Director, Administrative Group Co-ordinator, Corporate Sales Officer (the British are particularly keen on the 'officer' label) and even Group Manager's Liaison Executive. What

course, is busy with other matters, or he may be out playing golf, so he has assistants with impressive titles who will handle such things for him. A company which is placing a contract for, say, a new computer, doesn't want to deal with a mere salesman, so salesmen are Group Sales Executives or Sales Field Officers. Their seniors are Group Sales Managers and Regional Directors. American corporations make widespread use of the title 'vice-president'. It may not mean much – a large corporation can have twenty or thirty vice-presidents, reporting to senior vice-presidents – but it *sounds* important. Many VPs have little real power: their main job is to lunch with clients, make conference speeches and talk to is the Group Manager's Liaison Executive? Correct. He is the office boy – the 'lackey' who hands you the executive briefcase as you step into the Jaguar driven by the Personal Transport Assistant, or chauffeur.

If you don't have a department, you can always invent one. This is where concepts like Planning, Marketing and Research are so useful. The Head of Planning will naturally need a Deputy Head of Planning, an Assistant Deputy Head of Planning, a *Personal* Assistant to the Head of Planning, a dozen Planning Executives and a Head of Planning Liaison Executive – plus, of course, a Head of Planning Personal Transport Assistant, inevitably known as the HPPTA.

A major British corporation recently created the new post of 'Director of Human Resources'. Like everyone else, the executive who was given this impressive title is still trying to find out what it means. He *thinks* it is another way of saying 'Personnel Director', but the company *has* a Personnel Director. The answer is really quite simple: the brass of that particular corporation believe in giving people equal-sounding titles and leaving them to fight it out.

How to choose a corporate title:

Take any word from the first column, combine it with any word in the second column and add any word in the third column.

Senior	Group	Director
Deputy	Management	Officer
Acting	Sales	Co-ordinator
Assistant	Departmental	Head
Corporate	National	Supervisor
Managing	Divisional	Adviser
Administrative	Liaison	Operative
Personnel	Local	Assistant

YOUR OFFICE

The size of an executive's private office is not necessarily a reliable guide to his current standing in the corporation. Senior employees who have lost one battle too many, or who no longer have the stomach for corporate infighting, are often allowed to keep their plush offices – at least for a while – even though they have been deprived of any real power. It is a kind of consolation prize.

One American corporation has a special suite for executives who have ceased to play a significant role but who are clearly reluctant to accept the fact. It is lavishly furnished, but the desk is empty: he is no longer given anything to *do*. They hope that he will get the message before long and resign, but people like him often hang on for years.

Every executive naturally strives to get the largest office he can. It isn't easy because the competition is stiff and because incumbents tend to defend their territory with the ferocity of jungle animals. Most corporations have strict rules which govern not only the allocation of space but also the size and quality of carpets, curtains and desks. Juniors who press too hard are likely to be firmly rebuffed and their presumptuosness will earn them black marks. At the higher levels, the size of an executive's office is usually determined by his rank, but if he is appointed to a newly created post he may have to wait some time before a more impressive office becomes available. A good intelligence system can be of great help: a corporate infighter who hears, before everyone else, that another executive is leaving has the best chance of staking a claim to his domain before the rest do so.

But size is not the only thing that counts: *location* is often more important. We have already noted that most senior people tend to occupy the upper floors of the corporate HQ. It may well be advantageous to settle for a smaller office on the *right* floor. Try to get as close to the chief executive as possible, even if it means having to make do – for the time being – with comparatively modest accommodation.

Office furnishings are also significant. Even if you are not given a free choice in the matter of carpets and desk you can achieve a great deal by adding some carefully considered personal touches. If you do have a choice it pays to give a lot of thought to the kind of furnishings which will do the most for your image.

The starting point, obviously, is to decide what sort of image you want to project. Neat, efficient, all-business? Cosy, friendly, avuncular? Modern, progressive, trendy? Intellectual? Conformist?

People who run their own businesses can do pretty much what they like. (So can journalists and authors. Art Buchwald, the famous American humorist, has covered the walls of his office with framed 'hate mail' – letters from readers telling him what an awful man he is.) But corporation executives have to be more cautious. Eccentricity may have a certain charm but it can also be a barrier to promotion.

Avoid vulgar touches like calendars featuring nude females and holiday postcards from Florida, and resist the temptation to display cartoons which make fun of the company: they may get a laugh but are also likely to be taken as evidence that you don't take your employers seriously. Don't count on your superiors having a sense of humour.

Your desk should, if possible, be made of wood – preferably mahogany – rather than metal. Make sure it faces the door and place the visitor's chair in front of the desk, not beside it. (Some executives try to make callers feel inferior by choosing low, uncomfortable chairs. It is a well-known power ploy which invariably produces resentment. Why go out of your way to make enemies?) Filing cabinets and coffee-making machines indicate low status and should be banished to the outer office, along with typewriters. Desk computers are a different matter: they show that you recognize the importance of modern technology.

Indoor plants are acceptable, but avoid plastic flowers. Paintings should be original and convey good taste; *never* adorn your walls with posters advertising a bullfight or a play staged by the local amateur dramatic society.

Conference tables are a coveted symbol of rank; they show that the occupant is important enough to summon others to meetings. Many executives also have a separate area, with a coffee-table and couch, which can be used for informal discussions. The main problem with such arrangements is that it is often difficult to get a visitor to leave: he is so relaxed, so much at home, that he takes up an irritating amount of time – especially if one also offers him a drink.

The late Lord Beaverbrook solved the problem in a characteristically unorthodox fashion: he threw out *all* his cosy furniture and transacted his business standing up. People were in and out of his office in a matter of minutes. He got away with it because he was the boss; most of us have to resort to less offensive means. Some people have noisy wall clocks and make a point of casting anxious glances at them when they want visitors to go. A simpler but equally effective point is to arrange for one's secretary to come into the room and announce that one is overdue for another important appointment. Allocate, say, fifteen minutes for the meeting and then have her appear with a worried look on her face. If you want to continue the conversation, you can always impress your guest by telling her the appointment can wait. Alternatively, fit a buzzer to your desk so that she can be summoned whenever you wish to terminate the meeting.

Office Status Symbols

Large single-occupant room
Window and view
Computer console
Lined curtains
Wall-to-wall carpeting
Cocktail cabinet
Television set
Several telephones, including
    private telephone
Mahogany desk
Couch
Coffee table
Small, concealed refrigerator
Original paintings
Conference table with chairs
    around it
Bookcase
Private bathroom, with shower
Coffee served in china cups with
    saucer
Private lift
Own letterhead

Economist or *Financial Times* desk
    diary
Access to the executive dining
    room

Try to Avoid (or discard at the earliest opportunity)

Double or multi-occupant office
Metal desk
Anything made of plastic,
    especially flowers
Ashtrays stolen from hotel rooms
Posters
An overflowing in-tray (it suggests
    that you can't cope)
Stuffed fish
Coffee-maker (leave the coffee-
    making to your secretary)
Filing cabinet (ditto)
Framed diplomas from dubious
    institutions
Joke signs (people will think you
    are frivolous) and pretentious
    messages like 'the buck stops
    here' (it doesn't)
Calendars featuring nude females
Long-service citations from
    previous employers
Picture postcards from Florida
Photographs of the children
    (if you are constantly thinking of
    your family you can't be giving
    your full attention to the
    company's business)

"*Haven't you anything more
threatening?*"

You are what you're seen to be reading

People can tell a lot about you (or think they can) by the kind of publications they see in your office.

Newspapers, magazines and books can be useful props. You don't actually have to *read* them: what counts is that they should make a favourable impression.

You will naturally have the good sense to avoid working-class newspapers like the *Sun* and the *Daily Mirror* or magazines like *Playboy* and *Penthouse*. They should be kept at home, never in the office. And it is clearly foolish to stock your shelves with books which advertise your ambitions – titles like *Winning Through Intimidation* and Michael Korda's *Power! How to get it, how to use it.* (This book, too, should be kept out of sight. Why let rivals know that you are expert on corporate gamesmanship?)

The *Financial Times* is essential, especially for junior executives who want to show that they understand markets, and the *Economist* is widely used to suggest an intelligent interest in world affairs. Magazines like *Management Today* and *The Director* indicate that you have arrived – or are about to do so. If you work for an American-owned company, you should also display the European edition of the *Wall Street Journal* and magazines like *Fortune* and *Business Week*. Trade and professional journals show that you are keeping in close touch with events in your field.

Books on business and management should have long and boring titles: many people equate dullness with authority. Avoid books which criticize corporations or make fun of them, such as Anthony Sampson's *The Sovereign State of ITT*. It is perfectly all right, though, to display best-sellers like Alvin Toffler's *Future Shock* and *The Third Wave*. It shows that you are a forward-looking executive who keeps in touch with major trends.

Your desk diary should be large and prestigious, with leather-binding and your name or initials printed in gold letters. The *Financial Times* and *Economist* diaries are perfect.

YOUR SECRETARY

Choosing a secretary is one of the most important tasks you will ever undertake and it should be done with great care. A good secretary can make an executive look three times as good as he really is; an incompetent secretary represents a serious handicap.

Don't delegate the selection to any personnel officer or senior secretary, even if this is your company's custom. Insist on doing it yourself. Ideally, she should be brought in from outside; a second-hand secretary may have been spoiled by your predecessor. If you have to choose someone who is already working for the company, make a point of closely observing all the secretarial staff for a week or two. With luck, you should be able to spot someone who meets your requirements. You may have to use all your cunning to win her, but the effort is well worthwhile. Don't hesitate to steal her from her present boss, if you can. Many executives do not appreciate the crucial role of secretaries and discard them without giving the matter any serious thought; such foolish people don't deserve fair treatment. If they work for another company, so much the better.

A good secretary should have the following basic attributes:

She must be single – ideally widowed or divorced. You don't want someone who spends all her time on the telephone, chatting to boyfriends, or someone who has to rush home to take care of children. Let her work for others in the office; you can't afford her.

She must have an attractive personality. The last thing you want is an aggressive battle-axe who engages in daily combat with her colleagues. But she should *not* be beautiful. Many executives make the mistake of picking secretaries for their looks. The trouble with beautiful women is that they are also vain and easily distracted; men (including your own colleagues) are constantly hovering around her. You don't want divided loyalties. An 'old treasure' (see page 50) is often the best secret.

She must dress well, but not outrageously. Secretaries who flaunt their sexuality are a pain in the neck.

She must live within a reasonable distance from the office. If it takes her an hour or more to get home, she is likely to be a clock-watcher: she will be reluctant to work late. She is also liable to be persistently late in the mornings.

She must have a good memory. A secretary who forgets messages, or doesn't remember people's names,

can cause dreadful havoc.

She must be discreet. Office gossips are a menace: you don't want everyone else to know what you are up to. She should be a good listener (the company cafeteria is often a hidden reservoir of useful information), but she must be aware how easily your own interests could be damaged by careless talk.

She must be a competent actress. There are, inevitably, countless occasions when she will have to cover for you, to make excuses, to get rid of timewasters politely. This calls for considerable acting skills: a secretary who doesn't know how to do these things without giving offence can make you a lot of unnecessary enemies.

She must like her work. You don't want someone who does the job simply for the money or because she isn't qualified for anything else. Nor do you want one of those strident feminists who claim that secretarial tasks are demeaning and that the job they *really* think they deserve is yours. She is entitled to be ambitious, but let a rival cope with her. A good secretary takes pride in her work and accepts that it involves making her boss look the hero. She understands office warfare and is a loyal ally.

A two-way deal:

All partnerships require give and take; the boss-secretary relationship is no exception. If and when you have found your partner, try to remember these rules:

Don't treat her like a short-hand typist or call her 'your girl'. A proper secretary is as status-conscious as you are.

Let her know, from time to time, that you appreciate what she does for you. No one likes to be taken for granted.

Don't allow your wife to tell her what to do. She is there to help you in your job, not to run errands for the family. If you ask her to undertake some personal task, like cashing a cheque at the bank, view it as a favour rather than as an obligation.

Never reprimand or criticize her in the presence of others.

Don't make her work late unnecessarily. Some executives waste much of the day on trivial matters and then embark on a sudden burst of activity in the last half hour. Such thoughtless behaviour is bound to be resented: there should always be a reason for making her stay on.

Don't blame her for things which are really your fault. It's all too easy to say, 'My secretary got it wrong', but loyalty is supposed to be a two-way deal. If a mistake is likely to harm your career she will probably volunteer her services as a scapegoat. But let her volunteer.

Don't hold out on her. Make her aware of everything that is going on so that she can handle whatever may come up when you are not there.

| Don't lose your temper more than twice a week. When you do, have the good sense to say that you are sorry. | Don't keep threatening to fire her. She may take you at your word – and *then* where will you be? |

HOW TO GET MORE MONEY

The troops are paid wages and probably have a union which looks after their interests. The executive gets a salary and, although many corporations use a grading system, there is often considerable scope for negotiating a better deal.

Always remember the basic rule: if you don't ask, you don't get. But don't make the mistake of seeing things only from your point of view. The fact that you may be hard-pressed to pay your bills is of no concern to your employer: his job is to hire (and keep) the best possible talent at the most reasonable price. Try to assess what you may be worth to him and how keen he is to gain (or retain) your services.

Many executives operate on the principle that it is best to concentrate on securing promotion and letting the money side take care of itself. They fear that aggressive demands for more pay, without a corresponding increase in responsibility, are bound to be counter-productive. They have a point, but people who don't stand up for what they believe is right tend to be taken for granted and are often treated with contempt. The brass will never admit it, but there is a widespread feeling that executives who can't protect their own interests are unlikely to be much good at looking after the interests of the corporation.

The more information you have the better. You need to find out not only what your superiors think of you but also how much they are paying others in similar jobs and what the current market rate is. Most people are reluctant to discuss their salaries with colleagues, but you can usually get the answer by (a) pretending that you already know and (b) encouraging them to air their grievances over a drink after office hours. The market rate can be established by studying advertisements for executive jobs and by making inquiries among people who work for other companies. If the advertisements don't mention money you can always write and ask for details. It won't commit you to anything but you will get a good idea of what sort of figure you might command if you were to change employers.

Once you have done your homework you can start negotiations. If someone doing the same kind of job *is* being paid more, you can try appealing to your superior's sense of fairness. If the market rate *is* substantially above your present salary, you can make him aware of the fact and, if necessary, hint that you may leave. It helps, of course, if you already have a firm offer from another employer: it is, sadly, all too true that many companies appreciate an executive only when they are faced with the possibility that they might lose him. If you don't have a firm offer, play the 'I may leave' card only if you are sure that he would not wish you to do so.

Quiet, insistent repetition is the most effective technique you can use in asking for more money. When your superior raises an objection, say: 'I understand that. However, here is why I think this salary range is right/proper/correct. Never say: 'I don't agree' or 'That's wrong.' The name of the game is to persuade him that you have a strong case, not to arouse his anger.

If he mentions a figure, see if you can get him to go a bit higher. Research indicates that eighty per cent of the people who turn down the first salary offer get a second offer even if it is only a few hundred pounds more.

CREATIVE EXPENSE ACCOUNT MANAGEMENT

Every corporate infighter should have an expense account: it makes it so much easier to win friends and influence people. This has long been understood and accepted in countries like Japan, where expense account living sustains a huge service industry. Many American and European employers, alas, still take the old-fashioned view that it is a frivolous waste of the company's money. No wonder the Japanese so often defeat them in the battle for lucrative contracts.

The chairman naturally takes the view that any expenditure incurred by *him* is a worthwhile investment. So does the chief executive. The rest may have quite a job persuading the brass that they, too, should be allowed to make an 'investment'. The people most likely to succeed are those whose work calls for regular contact with outsiders: sales managers, advertising and marketing executives and public relations officers usually have the most generous expense accounts. Backroom boys find them harder to come by, which explains why accountants make so much trouble: they resent the fact that others are able to secure privileges which are denied to them and retaliate by being as awkward as possible. (Tax inspectors make difficulties for much the same reason.)

The best time to make your pitch is when you first join the company: the right to claim expenses should be negotiated as part of your service agreement. But don't be fobbed with a fixed allowance: its value will be eroded by inflation and it may be regarded as part of your overall remuneration package, which can cause problems when you ask for subsequent salary

70

A salesman who went on a business trip to Alaska lost £800 in a poker game. When he got home, he presented the following expense account claim:

Was lonely in Alaska, bought dog	£200
Dog was lonely, bought bitch	£200
Dog fell ill, medical expenses	£190
Dog died, funeral expenses	£180

The accountant added it all up and, delighted to have caught him out, exclaimed: 'But this comes to only £770!'

The salesman was equal to the challenge. 'Oh, I forgot,' he said. 'Flowers for bereaved bitch, £30.'

Moral: always make sure you get your sums right.

Another salesman returned from a visit to Rome. The accountant looked at his claim for expenses, and said: 'I can't pay this.'

The salesman knew that the company was doing badly and thought it advisable to make some concessions. 'Well,' he said, 'this bill for entertaining customers. I have claimed £150, but I must admit that a few people there were personal friends. I want to be reasonable – make it £100.'

'I am telling you,' the accountant said, 'I can't pay this.'

'Oh,' said the salesman. 'Well, this telephone bill for £80 – actually some of the calls I made were to home, so let's deduct £20.'

'The answer is still the same,' the accountant said. 'I can't pay this.'

'Oh dear,' said the salesman, by now thoroughly shaken. 'All right, this item here – £60 for a car and driver. Actually I drove myself, so let's say £40.'

'For the last time,' the exasperated accountant shouted, 'I can't pay this. *You haven't signed it.*'

Moral: always make sure that you get the formalities right.

increases. If you fail, try to manoeuvre yourself into a position which involves frequent meetings with people who might – just might – be useful to the company. If those meetings are abroad, so much the better. You will, of course, have to justify your expenditure and it is essential that you master the basic principles of what has become known as 'creative expense account management'.

One of the earliest exponents of the art was George Washington, who has been called 'the father of the expense account'. He laid down many of the principles still in use today. Example: be specific on the smaller expenditures and vague on the large ones. Describe in depth the purchase of a ball of twine, but casually throw in 'dinner for one army'.

Creative expense account management means thinking up ways of spending other people's money, rather than one's own, and Washington (who fought the entire revolution on expenses) was very good at it. The Japanese, who have learned so much from the Americans, also show a great deal of imagination. A favourite ploy is to invite an overseas visitor to have a night out in Tokyo's Ginza and use the occasion as an excuse for a monumental binge involving a dozen or more executives. No one complains; the brass, after all, habitually do the same.

Entertaining provides the most obvious scope, but you may also be able to persuade the company to pay your telephone bill (as a hard-working executive you naturally have to make a great many business calls from home), and it is a comparatively simple matter to create vaguely defined activities such as 'market studies' which require extensive travel at home and abroad.

It is important – indeed, vital – to make one's reasons sound as convincing as possible. Much of the cheating which goes on in large corporations is dangerously crass. Here are some of the common fiddles, known to every accountant:

Using fictitious names. You take your wife or girlfriend out to lunch and put her down as 'John Smith' or 'Bill Jones'. A foolish move, because you may be spotted (and denounced) by a rival.

Using a bus and claiming the taxi fare. Easily done, but petty. Why risk trouble for small change?

Accepting an invitation to lunch or dinner and then claiming that you, rather than your host, paid the bill. You may get away with it – until your boss, who has signed your expenses, meets the host and discovers the truth.

Buying fake bills from a waiter. Some people think this is rather clever: one gives him a tip and he hands over bills left behind by other customers, which one can use to support one's claims. But waiters talk and there is a very real risk that he will tell others about it.

Claiming expenses for trips that were never made. Another fraud that is all too easily exposed by someone who is really determined to do so – which he will be if he suspects that one is a habitual cheat.

Moral issues apart, the problem with this kind of fiddling is that the person doing it not only stands to lose his expense account but also his job: an employer is fully justified in dismissing him on the spot and letting everyone know why he has taken such a drastic step. There is no need for such stupid greed: the imaginative executive should be able to find plenty of legitimate excuses for making the most of an expense account.

"Of course it's on business, tell him 'miscellaneous' of his expense account is here."

THE GOLDEN HANDSHAKE

Some executives have become experts in the art of extracting large sums of money from their employers by playing the 'golden handshake game'. The rules are simple: you arrange to be offered another job, but don't tell anyone. You then make life so impossible for your superiors that they will fire you. If you have a service contract, they will generally pay you handsome compensation – if only to keep you quiet. A week later you start work for the other corporation.

It is a ploy which has paid off many a mortgage. The people who play it usually justify it with the argument that employers regularly hand out shabby treatment to their staff – this is one way of hitting back. Besides, they say, the brass can afford it.

Most of us, of course, wouldn't dream of joining in. We like our present jobs too much, don't approve of cheating and regard being fired as an act of public

73

humiliation. If we have to leave, we would much rather resign. Employers are usually quite willing to let us take the resignation route, because it avoids embarrassment for all concerned and is a good deal cheaper. The humiliation factor is their strongest card: few executives can bear the thought of being exposed as people the corporation no longer wants or needs. It's like being drummed out of the regiment.

The handshake players are made of sterner stuff. Getting the sack, they argue, no longer carries the stigma it once did. It happens to many able people when times are bad, and when they are good. Everyone knows that losing a job is not necessarily due to incompetence or misdemeanour. It may happen because of a merger, or because the employer has lost an important contract, or because a new venture hasn't turned out to be as profitable as the company hoped it would be. Sometimes people are fired on a whim. When Henry Ford II told his president, Lee Iaccoca, to pack his bags, Iaccoca asked what he had done wrong. Ford's answer: 'I just don't like you.' (Iaccoca, of course, collected a big cheque and soon afterwards took over at Chrysler, where he has become a conspicuous success.) So, the players say, it is stupid to resign and relinquish your claim to severance pay.

They have a point, but there obviously is a considerable difference between being 'let go' when you are quite happy to stay and engineering your own dismissal. The unwilling victim has a moral – as well as a legal – claim against his employers, unless he has been turfed out because of proven dishonesty. The player is merely an opportunist trying to exploit employers who, in many cases, have always treated him fairly and decently.

You will have your own views on the subject, but it is worth dealing, briefly, with some of the steps you can and should take to protect your interests.

Get a service contract:

Chief executives don't really like handing out service contracts, except for themselves. But many companies have found, in recent years, that they have to make a commitment of this sort if they want to attract – and keep – the best people. As in the case of expense accounts, the most favourable time to ask for a service contract is at the time you join. It is generally more difficult to get one if you have already been with the company for several years, but if a newcomer doing much the same job has managed to secure a contract you are entitled to demand equal treatment. Try to find out.

Don't resign:

The players are right about this – it's stupid to resign if you don't want to go and if you have done nothing wrong. Let them fire you and demand adequate compensation. The fact that so many people are able to land good jobs elsewhere shows that prospective employers won't necessarily hold it against you.

If you do agree to resign, rather than allowing yourself to be fired, persuade your employers to let you write your own announcement, one that will make you look good. Not everyone will believe it, but most people will readily accept what you say – after all, it happens all the time.

Work out your notice:

It is tempting to leave right away – to clear out your desk and be gone. Your employer may insist on it and, as long as he pays you proper compensation, there is no point in fighting him. But hang in there if you can. It gives you a better image if people are still able to contact you at a business address and job-hunting is much easier if you have the use of a desk, a telephone and perhaps a secretary.

Ask your boss for help:

Don't be too proud to ask your employer if he knows of anyone else who might be able to use your services. Give him an opportunity to be nice: you'll need all the contacts you can get. Firing people is an unpleasant business – most top managers hate doing it – and one can usually count on getting at least some co-operation.

Only the press talks about people being 'fired'; corporations prefer to use more gentle terms. They 'let them go' or 'terminate their services'. Mass sackings are invariably called 'releasing surplus labour'.

People are not 'unemployed' either. They are 'disemployed', 'in the process of redeployment', 'resting', or 'involuntarily leisured'. In China, they are said to be 'awaiting reassignment'.

Everyone knows the truth, of course, but euphemisms sound so much more pleasant. They take some of the sting out of being fired.

You, too, can play the game if (God forbid) you should lose your job. Tell everyone that you are 'seeking fresh challenges' or 'exploring new opportunities' or 'pursuing personal interests'.

"He used to be very high-powered. He was replaced by two silicon chips!"

A LITTLE SUGAR

If you never have been offered a bribe you may feel vaguely insulted; it suggests that no one has thought you worth bribing. But look on the bright side: you might have been tempted to accept and *that* could have meant trouble.

It is quite common for executives to receive small bribes – a case of Scotch at Christmas, a gold fountain pen, a free trip abroad. No one ever calls them 'bribes', of course. They are gifts; harmless (so it's said) acts of generosity. But the motive is generally much the same as that behind big bribes: the people who send them hope that they will create goodwill and lead to orders. The aim is to create an obligation on the part of the recipient.

The borderline between a bribe and a genuine business gift – between corruption and the proper oiling of the wheels of commerce – is indefinable. As a former British Lord Chief Justice once remarked: 'Corruption is like a sausage – hard to describe, but easy enough to smell.' This is why many

corporations forbid their executives to accept gifts of any kind, though in practice no one worries about trifles like desk diaries and calendars. Others leave it to their executives to make their own judgement.

If you are doing business with one of the many countries where bribery is part of the way of life, it may give offence if you return the gift. Many people prefer to keep it and hope that no one will find out, rather than risk upsetting a valuable contact. But it is often better to play safe: this is an area of business life where Looking After Number One requires considerable caution. Say that you appreciate the gesture, but that the company's regulations prohibit you from taking it. If there are no rules, blame the law.

In general, one's attitude should be ruled by common sense. Very few corporations will sack an executive who accepts a case of Scotch. The trouble arises if you accept something more substantial, such as a handsome cheque.

Large bribes are not called by that name either: they are usually described as 'commissions'. When the Lockheed scandal hit the headlines in the 1970s, one of the company's officials used an even more cosy label: 'sugar'. The practice was defended, at the time, on the grounds that the end justified the means. If payola could secure sales, then it was cheap at the price. 'In certain parts of the world,' the London *Times* noted, 'the businessman is faced with a simple choice. Either he allows a bribe to be paid, or he does not get the business.' The same argument is still widely used today, though many corporations insist that they do not approve of such behaviour. The people who work in those 'certain parts of the world' may see nothing wrong with taking bribes – indeed, they demand them – but the same does not apply in countries like the United States and Britain. The executive who accepts a bribe is not only breaking his company's rules (which justifies instant dismissal) but also risks prosecution.

No doubt some manage to get away with it. There are always people who believe in chancing their arm. But it is a dangerous game, not least because of the possibility of blackmail. Don't play it.

STRATEGIC
WARDROBE
MANAGEMENT

'YOU ARE WHAT YOU WEAR'

If, as it is often said, nothing succeeds like the appearance of success, the way you dress is clearly important. There are some basic rules for female executives on page 108; this section is primarily concerned with what will – and will not – help the male corporate infighter.

There have been great changes on the business fashion scene in the past century and even over the last few decades. Clothes – and accessories – which used to be regarded as essential for success nowadays look absurd. If you turned up at the office looking like J.P. Morgan or John D. Rockefeller, people would laugh. It does not necessarily mean that modern fashions are better; they are, quite simply, different.

People in glamour industries like films and television can afford to be outrageous – indeed, it generally pays to advertise one's individuality. The entrepreneur who runs his own company can also please himself, though in practice he tends to be very conscious of the likely reaction of the people he does business with. The executive working for a large corporation has far less freedom: he is expected to dress in a manner approved by the brass, which is why corporation men all tend to look much the same. Their wives may prefer them to look like the handsome models in *Playboy*, but high fashion is frowned upon. If you were to turn up at the office in a smart leather jacket and a turtle-neck pullover, you would be regarded as one of those dangerous people who have no respect for convention and would probably be told never to do it again.

Sobriety and respectability have traditionally been represented by dullness and drabness, and that still applies today. It is widely assumed that a man who dresses in a 'businesslike' manner is competent and trustworthy. The opposite may be true, of course. Wearing the 'right' clothes doesn't make one competent, and some of the most 'businesslike' dressers have turned out to be con-men. The tailor has always been indispensable to the swindler.

Some corporations have formal dress codes (they would probably be happiest if they could put everyone into a corporate uniform) but most tend to make do with unwritten rules. There is an 'understanding' that executives should wear clothes which will identify them as members of the corporate team, not clothes that will single them out.

The guru of the business world, as far as dress is concerned, is John T. Molloy, who in 1976 wrote a best-seller called *Dress for Success*. Molloy – dubbed 'America's first wardrobe engineer' by *Time* magazine – insisted that 'in matters of clothing, conservative, class-conscious conformity is absolutely essential to the success of the American business and professional man'. His advice is still taken as gospel in many corporations. He laid down, for example, that 'the proper colours for a gentleman's suit are blue and grey'. Recent statistics show that blue and grey account for more than half of all the suits sold in America.

Many fashion writers have challenged his edicts – they seem to have been particularly incensed by his declaration that brown suits are inappropriate attire for climbing the corporate ladder. But the 'wardrobe engineer' is unrepentant and he continues to have enormous influence.

Dress for Success is well worth reading, but you only have to look around you to see what corporations regard as right and wrong. You may feel the urge to rebel, but it pays not to go too far. Strategic wardrobe management means studying what the chairman, the chief executive and the other key figures are wearing and more or less following their lead. You will be regarded as 'one of us' rather than 'one of them'.

The business suit:

Suits still predominate and you should have four or five – more if you can afford them. They should obviously include blue or grey solids (black is also a good colour if you need to transmit more authority) and narrow pinstripes. (Broad stripes are liable to make you look like a Chicago gangster.) Waistcoats should be worn only by people who are slim. Braces are definitively out; always wear a belt.

Shirts:

White is still the favourite colour, followed by pale blue. Businessmen have become more daring in their choice of shirts – one now sees a greater variety of colours and patterns than in the past – but it is still advisable to avoid gaudy colours (don't wear solid red or green) and to choose stripes rather than dots or floral and paisley patterns.

We have, mercifully, escaped from the tyranny of stiff collars, but many people like to wear white collars with striped blue shirts. It can look very smart, but make sure that the collar is always spotlessly clean.

Shoes:

Black, all leather shoes are the standard corporate footwear. Brown is also acceptable, providing it doesn't clash with the colour of the suit. Some businessmen are fond of suede shoes, but they tend to look rather scruffy after a short time. Avoid multi-coloured shoes, tassels and gaudy buckles.

Pullovers:

You shouldn't need them. Most offices are well-heated, and if you go out on a cold day you should be wearing a smart overcoat. Knitted pullovers (especially those with strong patterns) have a working-class image and should never be worn by an ambitious executive. An expensive-looking cardigan is better, but is still regarded as much too casual. Never wear one for a meeting: the proper attire for a meeting is a suit.

BIG IS SUCCESSFUL

Tall men are generally more successful in the corporate world than those who are short; they convey more authority. You may also find it comforting to hear that being overweight is no barrier to reaching the top. The reverse may be true.

A team of researchers established, not long ago, that even in diet-conscious America the key positions are occupied by men who are 'heavy' – a euphemism for 'fat'. The team found that 'if two men were alike, except for the fact that one was overweight, the fatter could expect to earn a third more than the skinny one'.

It may well be that they acquired the fat on the way up; by the time they got there it no longer mattered *what* shape they were. But fat men generally feel more at ease in the presence of other fatties and this may make them more inclined to promote them.

The trouble with men who look like nature's toothpicks is that they make others feel guilty. Corporate leaders don't want to be constantly reminded that their wives and doctors are right to nag them about their weight. People who are always dieting tend to be even worse: they are insufferably smug about their little victories ('I lost another four pounds this week') and are usually poor company. It is hard to establish a reasonable relationship with someone who insists that lunch should consist of cottage cheese, a few lettuce leaves and a glass of water. Dieting also tends to make people miserable and bad-tempered, which very easily leads to the conclusion that they 'don't get on' with other members of the corporate team.

So don't worry if you are overweight; it may be a blessing. Try to make sure, though, that you won't be regarded as a slob. People may accept the extra pounds, but they won't accept a slovenly appearance. Don't wear clothes that are too tight (fat men should always go to a good tailor) and try to be well-groomed. You don't have to feel guilty about that bulging tummy, but you don't have to advertise it either. And there really is *no* excuse for ill-fitting and badly-pressed suits, gravy-stained ties and dirty shirts.

ACCESSORIES

Because the need to conform tends to make all executives look alike, accessories have become vitally important. People *expect* you to appear in a blue or grey suit; they will only notice what you wear if you don't. They do, however, keep a sharp eye on all the details which make one executive a little different from another: the attaché case, the watch, the pen, the credit card, and so on. Choosing the right accessories therefore requires great care.

Attaché cases:

Every executive should have an attaché case; it is not only functional but also identifies you as a decision-maker. Avoid large cases: you don't want to be mistaken for an encyclopaedia salesman. The best are small or medium-sized, and made of top quality leather. (A rich dark-brown is ideal.) It should be plain and simple, but expensive-looking. Monograms are acceptable, but should not be brash.

Attaché cases should be used to carry documents, files and perhaps a calculator; *never* your lunch. Go through it regularly and weed out all the junk which has accumulated during the week.

Some manufacturers nowadays sell very fancy products: there is, for example, a 'secret connection' case lined with bullet-proof fabric and equipped with items like a miniature voice stress analyser (to let you know when someone is lying), a pocket recorder which picks up conversations up to fifty feet or more a way, a high-powered walkie-talkie with built-in scrambler, a bomb sniffer and even a pocket 'nite vision scope', which allows you to see in total darkness. It seems to be primarily designed for paranoid chairmen and executives who have an irresistible urge to play James Bond. *You* don't need it.

Jewellery:

Forget about tie-pins (they are old-fashioned) and baubles like ID bracelets (they are considered effeminate). The basic rule about men's jewellery is: the less the better. Cuff links are OK, providing they are small and simple: big, ostentatious cuff-links will make you look like a Mafioso. Don't wear more than one ring (wedding rings are acceptable, though you risk being regarded as hen-pecked). Belt buckles, too, should be small and elegant.

Wallets:

The trouble with wallets is that one tends to put too much in them; the result is an unsightly bulge in the jacket of one's suit. Most items can be carried just as easily (and less obtrusively) in your attaché case. If you must have a wallet, make sure that it is slim – avoid temptation – and keep the contents down to the bare minimum: credit cards, business cards, a little cash.

Handkerchiefs:

Stick to plain white. Coloured handkerchiefs, or handkerchiefs that match ties, may look all right in the breast pocket of your suit (though they should never be made a prominent feature) but don't use them to blow your nose.

Pocket diaries:

Many companies give away pocket diaries at Christmas – top executives generally receive far more than they need. They are obviously helpful and conspicuous consultation of your diary will do much to make you look the part of the sought-after, time-pressured businessman. But if you use one of these freebies be sure that it is leather-bound and that the company's name (usually displayed on the cover) is a prestigious one.

Credit cards:

Credit cards are now so common

that they have ceased to be a status symbol. People will comment only on the *absence* of a credit card: if you pay for lunch with cash you will look like one of those poor fellows who cannot be trusted with a charge account. If you want to impress others, you must have one or more 'gold cards'. These are issued by major hotel chains, car rental firms, top stores and the credit card companies themselves and advertise your status as an affluent and valued customer.

Watches:

Watches tell more than the time – some go 'beep' to remind you to take a pill, or that you are overdue for a business meeting; some check your heartbeat; some have a built-in lie detector. They also tell people what kind of a person you think you are. Avoid watches designed for skin-divers and astronauts, and have nothing to do with the 'fun' watches sold in so many stores. A Mickey Mouse watch may amuse the secretaries in the office, but your superiors will be appalled: you will, not surprisingly, be regarded as a man who has yet to grow up. The best kind of watch for an ambitious executive is thin, plain and gold, with a leather band.

Pens:

Many people are careless about pens: they don't mind what kind they use as long as it does the job. But a cheap, half-chewed ball-point pen makes a terrible impression. If you don't want to be thought of as a slob (and who does?) buy a trim metal ball-point sheathed in plated gold or silver. They are not expensive, so it doesn't really matter very much if

one gets lost or stolen.

Umbrella:

Many executives still regard the umbrella as an essential part of the corporate uniform – an accessory which should be carried whenever one ventures out into the street, even in blazing sunshine. It tends to look pretty silly on a beautiful day in California, or anywhere else, and more and more people take the sensible view that it should be treated as merely another piece of equipment, useful in countries with an unpredictable climate (and for hailing taxis) but by no means indispensable. A smart raincoat will, after all, do just as well.

If you buy an umbrella, choose the standard type – black, with a plain handle. Leave the golf umbrellas to the golfers and the multi-coloured versions to the tourists.

Hats:

Hats are no longer *de rigueur*, even in the most conservative financial institutions. Soviet cartoonists still like to portray Western businessmen as wicked capitalists in top hats, but top hats are rarely worn nowadays except at weddings and social functions like Ascot. The same has become increasingly true of other familiar headgear like the British bowler; most executives regard them as out of date and wouldn't be seen dead in one. Texan oil-millionaires (and would-be millionaires) still seem to be fond of Stetsons, but New Yorkers – and most other Americans – think they look ridiculous. Black 'dudes' like to wear those wide-brimmed, soft-felt hats which were so popular in the 1920s but the business world tends to associate them with gangsters (blame all those movies) and executives avoid them like the plague.

Don't expect a hat – *any* hat – to do anything for your image. It is far better to be bare-headed and risk the occasional cold.

Business cards:

It is essential to have an ample supply of business cards: if you don't, people will assume that you are unimportant. But exercise modesty in choosing the printed size of your name: don't be vulgar. Steer clear of trite business slogans like 'Hi, my name is John Smith – Mobile Comfort Stations is the name of the game'. Go for a discreet logotype on a card of modest dimensions. In addition to your name, title, business and address, it should have your telephone and telex number. Adding a translation in, say, Japanese will convey the impression that you are a much-travelled executive with a wide range of contacts.

The style in which you present your card is also significant. Don't dish them out like a demented confetti machine: it is bad form and you may regret giving it to all and sundry. Cards should always be exchanged at the end of a discussion with people you genuinely expect to do business with.

HAIR

Never mind what wives and girlfriends say: most corporations like their male employees to have short, neat hair. In Victorian days businessmen sprouted an extraordinary variety of facial hair – beards, mutton-chop whiskers, drooping moustaches. All that ceased to be fashionable a long time ago.

Some people still cling to the view that beards are a sign of strength and manhood, but in the world of finance and business only the portraits of the founding fathers can wear them without attracting disapproving frowns from the people around the Boardroom table. Top men do not wear beards (even royals like Prince Philip and Prince Charles would not dream of doing so). In the 1980s, beards are associated with dangerous revolutionaries and anarchists; blame Fidel Castro.

Much the same is true of long hair. It may be sexy, but the long-haired executive is liable to be regarded as an extremist, an unwelcome advocate of unconventional ideas.

Mutton-chop whiskers look ridiculous, and long sideburns are considered effeminate. If you must have a moustache, keep it moderate. No handlebars and no thin pencil stripes.

Crew cuts are acceptable, but it is far better to opt for the smart, well-trimmed, inconspicuous executive look. Keep your hair tidy at all times, but *don't* make a habit of combing it in the middle of a meeting. Do all you can to avoid dandruff.

Grey hair looks distinguished, but in corporations where the emphasis is on youthful leadership it may be advisable to keep the greying process in check by the skilful use of dye. White hair only works at the Boardroom level and even there it can be a handicap: it is a constant reminder that, perhaps, it is time you were sent into retirement.

Wigs and toupees are a problem. They make one look younger, but sooner or later word will spread that you are wearing one and people will start to make jokes about it. There is much to be said for doing without such aids; if you are going bald, it is probably a good idea to tell people, aggressively, that baldness is a sign of virility.

Smoking

If in doubt, put it out. Or never light up in the first place. The opposition to smoking has become increasingly virulent – and there is no more virulent opponent than the chairman or chief executive who has given it up. Some corporations have banned smoking in the office, especially in America, and many will not hire people who smoke during the interview or who have nicotine-stained fingers. The cigarette smoker, especially, is liable to incur the enmity of nearly everyone around him. A chain-smoker is reckoned to be an unstable character as well as a damned nuisance.

In some of the private executive dining rooms, cigars are still offered at the end of lunch. If the host takes one, it may seem safe to do the same. But some of the other guests may object: it is, on the whole, safer to decline. Never put a cigar in your pocket so that you can smoke it later (it's bad form) and under no circumstances produce a pipe. Wait until you get home.

THE COMPANY TIE

Companies ties are much in evidence these days: many corporations believe that they boost morale, by giving employees a comforting feeling of 'belonging', and are a cheap but effective form of advertising. They generally display the company logo and are the corporate equivalent of the regimental tie, or old school tie. Some are embarrassingly vulgar and many employees, especially senior executives, hate the sight of them. But it is advisable not to make the brass aware of one's contempt for this dubious symbol of togetherness.

The British may not have invented ties, but they can certainly claim to have pioneered tie snobbery. It has long been a fashionable way to publicize elitism. The regimental tie does not carry the status it once did but it is still popular, especially among bankers and stockbrokers who once served in the Guards. The same is true of the old school tie. If you have been to Eton or Harrow, and want to make others aware of the fact, a tie is the obvious answer. In a class-conscious society it instantly proclaims that the wearer comes from the 'right sort of background'. There are university ties, civil service ties, teaching hospital ties and, of course, club ties. Scotland Yard has a tie for each department and there are even trade union ties.

In America, too, the tie is an important denominator of social status. A Harvard, Yale or Princeton is rated far more highly than a mere company tie and most corporate infighters consider it to be a major asset.

A word of warning, though. One should *never* wear a tie to which one is not entitled. Nothing is more likely to infuriate a genuine Etonian or Harvard man than an outsider's blatant attempt to pass himself off as one of them. It simply isn't done. The risk of detection is high and, once the wearer has been

"Actually, it started off as a think tank!"

exposed, word will get around in no time at all. He will henceforth be known as a liar – and a clumsy liar at that.

There are, of course, all kinds of other ties. Some salesman, for example, like to wear a Concorde tie. They think it impresses the customers. It may well do so, providing one has actually *flown* on Concorde and can describe what it is like. Then there are the various wildlife ties. A few years ago, the 'Save the Whale' campaign tie was fashionable for a while. Unfortunately, most of the people who wore them knew nothing about the whales and, it soon transpired, had no real interest in the efforts to save them. Executives also found that such ties involved the risk of being regarded as environmental freaks – one of the sworn enemies of large corporations – and hastily consigned them to the wastepaper basket. Others, mostly in the junior ranks, were foolish enough to wear those silly male chauvinist pig ties, which made them unnecessary enemies among female colleagues and influential secretaries.

The safest course, if one doesn't qualify for a prestigious tie, and there isn't a company tie, is to stick to one of the many types which have always found acceptance in the business world – solid blue or grey silk ties, and ties with polka dots or diamonds. They convey respectability and responsibility.

Bow ties? There is a school of thought which suggests that people who wear bow ties cannot be taken seriously; that they cannot be trusted with anything important. I am sure it will come as news to Sir Robin Day, but I dare say that there is some truth in it.

EYEGLASSES

Many executives hate wearing glasses: they think it is a sign of weakness. But they really have no need to worry. Most of the top men in the corporation probably wear them too. Nothing is worse than pretending to be able to do without them – and ending up peering short-sightedly at important documents or, worse, ignoring important people one may meet in the office corridors.

Glasses can be a useful asset. They make most people look more serious, more respectable. They also help young executives to look older. Glasses can be used, in meetings, to underline a point – giving it extra weight – or to gain time to consider an awkward question. A common ploy is to take them off, wipe them carefully while one considers what to say, and then wave them at the man who has asked the awkward question while giving one's answer.

But one must choose the right type of glasses. A cheap wire frame won't do; it makes you look like an impoverished junior clerk. Nor will dark, tinted glasses; everyone will think you are a Mafioso. A monocle is clearly absurd. The most sensible approach is to decide what personality one wants to project and select an appropriate frame. Heavy, horn-rimmed glasses convey authority. (But avoid black.) A gold frame can look very elegant but may be regarded as ostentatious. Men with swarthy complexions should choose light frames; it will make them less sinister.

If you are getting on in years, and want to disguise the fact, you may, of course, prefer to wear contact lenses. Many political leaders do so.

HOW
TO WIN
MEDALS

WINNING MEDALS

T here are many ways of winning medals on the corporate battlefield, but being modest is *not* one of them. It isn't enough to pull off a coup: you have to make sure that the people who count in the corporation get to hear about it.

This often requires considerable subtlety. Your superiors won't appreciate brashness and they certainly don't want their subordinates to go over their heads to the chief executive or one of the other members of the general staff. They prefer to take the credit themselves. (While, of course, being swift to blame you when things go wrong.) It is usually better to let someone else – an ally – make appropriate efforts on your behalf. You can do the same for him.

There are, however, occasions when an executive is given a chance to focus attention on himself. He may be asked to make a presentation at a meeting of the brass, or he may be invited to speak at a seminar or even a convention. If this should happen to you, give it all you've got. Nothing is worse than having to listen to someone who clearly hasn't done his homework and who, as a result, stumbles through his act with an obvious lack of self-confidence.

There is a story about an IBM executive who had to make a presentation to the then chairman and chief executive. He arrived with an armful of papers, which he put – one by one – on the great man's desk. The chairman was in a bad mood that morning and, after listening impatiently for a few minutes, swept the lot onto the floor. The executive calmly got down on his knees, gathered up the documents, and said: 'Okay, I presume you prefer that I continue my presentation from here.' And that's exactly what he did.

The fellow, you will admit, had style. Most presentations take a rather more orthodox form, but if you encounter an irascible boss you must know what to do.

Countless boring studies prove that we absorb information least rapidly and thoroughly through the ear, better through the eye, and best of all through the Disney combination of sound and vision. This is why so many executives nowadays make extensive use of audio-visual aids – slides, tapes and videos. Computer graphs are always impressive, even if no one understands them.

Seminars and conventions have increasingly become what is known as 'Industrial Theatre'. Talking is not considered enough; the aim, nowadays, is to create a dramatic impetus for the event so that the informational content may become both easier to assimilate and more likely to be remembered. The speaker's entrance is preceded by carefully-selected mood music and attention-grabbing flashing lights, followed by an expertly produced slide or video presentation, spectacular audio-visual modules ('The Romance of Wholesale Plumbing Supplies'), sketches with professional actors, guest appearances by famous television personalities, and even troupes of hip-swinging disco dancers.

Not surprisingly, a kind of conference folklore has begun to emerge among veteran suppliers of these services – a collection of tall tales and untrustworthy anecdotes. They tell of the VIP guest speaker who was unable to deliver a lecture entitled 'Man, Master of the Universe' because the slide projector jammed; the company manufacturing duplicating machines whose joint managing directors turned out to be identical twins; the nationwide chain of discount stores whose meetings always ended with two-and-a-half cheers for the chairman; the microphone which bent over as Uri Geller collected his thoughts before a banquet speech; and the travel agent in a small Italian town who took delegates on a tour of the local beauty spots and whose brother made a tour of the hotel rooms, on behalf of the Mafia, while they were enjoying the sights.

Cynics have offered various definitions of 'conferences' and some are worth repeating:

A conference is an arrangement, blessed by the taxman, by which people are able to take their holidays in the company of other persons whom they see every day of the year.

A conference is primarily a means of enabling people with some common interest to present a united front against the outside world.

A conference is a gathering of people who singly can do nothing, but together can decide that nothing can be done.

A conference is an institution for getting people together and telling them what they believe, and why they believe it, while all around them they have the feeling that all the other people who matter believe it too.

The last one probably comes closest to the truth. The annual conferences of large corporations like IBM are, above all, a mass affirmation of the credo that the corporation is a wondrous entity, and that higher sales and profits are the most important thing on earth.

IBM even used to have its own songs. Its management is now rather shame-faced about them and they are rarely heard, but a brief extract from one will give you the flavour:

> March on with IBM. We lead the way!
> Onward we'll ever go, in strong array

Our thousands to the fore, nothing can stem
Our march forever more, with IBM.

March on with IBM. Work hand in hand,
Stout-hearted men go forth, in every land
Our flags on every shore, we march with them
On high forever more, for IBM.

Some of the stout-hearted men must have found it hard to remain serious. But, whatever the reason for a conference, it gives high-fliers the chance to shine. Make the most of it.

MAKING A SPEECH

Most executives become different people when they ascend a platform: he who talks so much down-to-earth common sense in the bar is often a pompous bore when he makes a speech.

You may have had a drink with him beforehand and discussed the state of your company's order book and the foolishness of economists. His language then was blunt and direct. Up there on the platform, though, he is another person. He no longer tries to say what he thinks, but falls back on dreary platitudes. We must, he says, get the country going again. End frustration.

Reward enterprise. Meet the challenge of the eighties. And so on.

Many businessmen manage to sail through countless conferences, at home and abroad, by using a simple recipe. Take half a dozen quotes from long-forgotten political speeches, add a few generalizations, stir in a few jokes and flattering comments about the host and audience, and serve in a breezy manner. If they are addressing people from their own company, they congratulate everyone on their achievements, thank the wives for their support, mention the importance of profits, and urge them to try harder still.

The chairman or chief executive may get away with it – he is listened to with respect even when he is talking the most awful rubbish. You cannot count on the same treatment and should not do so. If you waffle you will, inevitably, be written off as someone who has nothing to contribute. The audience will be appalled by your lack of depth. Your reputation will suffer and you almost certainly will not be asked to speak again.

It usually pays to stick to the topics you know best. That may seem obvious, but you would be surprised how many people chance their luck in areas they know no better than the next man. You are much more likely to impress an audience if you specialize. Your experience and knowledge of the subject will come through, and you will be able to challenge conventional thinking without making people angry. You will also be able to work in some neat little plugs for your own triumphs and pet schemes.

To do this, of course, you should try to get as much information as possible about the aims and framework of the conference, and about the kind of people who are expected to attend. Insist on certain details, no matter how hard-pressed the organizers may be. There is a world of difference between addressing fifty people and five hundred, and between an audience of fellow experts and one of laymen. What is the rest of the programme and how do you relate to it? Precisely what does the programme committee hope to accomplish? *Who* will be there? Will there be questions afterwards?

The pitfalls are legion. Programme committees have a penchant for thinking up smart, but misleading, titles. Or they will be deliberately vague because no one has ever decided what the conference is *about*. Do your homework and be prepared to change your speech to suit the mood of the occasion.

Dale Carnegie, author of one of the best books on public speaking, said that 'the gaining of self-confidence and courage, and the ability to think calmly and clearly while talking to a group, is not one tenth as difficult as most people imagine.' Most of the great orators in history, he pointed out, were nervous when they first faced an audience. Lloyd George was 'in a state of misery . . . my tongue clung to the roof of my mouth, and at first I could hardly get out a word'. Disraeli confessed that he would rather have led a cavalry charge than to have to face the House of Commons; his opening speech was a ghastly failure. There is no reason why a good engineer, accountant or production manager should automatically be a good speaker. It takes training and practice to do really well. But if you know your subject well, and have worked out what you are going to say, you have a very good chance of making a favourable impression.

Do's and don'ts of public speaking:

Don't start a speech with an apology. If you tell an audience that you are 'not used to this sort of thing' you will make everybody nervous and embarrassed. Don't ask for sympathy; set out to impress them.

Don't make jokes about the top management, unless they are flattering. Rival companies make a more acceptable target. Never tell risqué stories. They may be very funny, but some of the people in the audience (most likely the chairman or chief executive) are sure to take offence.

Don't be a windbag. People who drone on for hours, without really saying anything, are the bane of every seminar and convention. Say what you have to say, and try to make it as concise and interesting as possible. Ask yourself: how would I respond to a bore?

Don't write down every word of a speech and then proceed to read in a dull monotonous voice. You will send everyone to sleep. Write notes on stout cards, judge the mood of your audience, and vary your pace.

Don't devote the *entire* speech to self-praise. Work in a few commercials (and back them with facts) but remember that there are others who think they are just as good as you are and would like to hear it acknowledged. If you think they don't deserve it, praise the company.

Don't end too abruptly. Brevity is fine, but don't slam on the brakes. Thank your host – and the audience for listening.

Do rehearse a slide presentation. Many a performance has been wrecked by the casual handling of visual material. If your slides or film material come out at the wrong time the audience will roar with laughter and you will be left standing there, red-faced and desperate to regain control of the situation.

Do go easy on the booze. One Scotch will relax you; three can make you incoherent. You may not notice it at the time, but everyone else will – and when you sober up you will be *mortified*.

Do remember to be optimistic. You may not feel it, but it pays to project a positive, upbeat image.

Do learn how to use a microphone. Check it before the function starts; you don't want a lot of hiccups and burps just as you get going. Make sure that it doesn't hide your face; adjust it so that people can see your eyes. Don't speak too close to it and don't clutch it as if it were a life-belt.

Do control your gestures. They should not be confused with gesticulation; gesture in a speech must add emphasis to the words.

Do try to be polite at question time, even if someone attacks the points you've made. He is entitled to his opinion. A calm, rational reply shows that you know how to keep cool under pressure.

Going on TV

Few interviews for news and current affairs programmes last more than three or four minutes – often not even that. So don't arrive with an armful of briefing papers, determined to make a speech. You are expected to make crisp, emphatic statements. If the interview is edited, they will almost certainly be the only bits they use.

Remember that on television how you *look* is at least as important as what you say. The camera will pick up every expression, so try not to appear woolly, shifty, indecisive. A good performer comes across as sincere (even when he isn't) and authoritative.

If you make an in-house video, keep it short – fifteen minutes should generally be the maximum. Show your face, by all means, but don't overdo it. You don't want people to think that you are vain. Use plenty of visual material and record a 'voice-over' commentary. Don't lecture; get your message across as simply – and firmly – as possible.

QUALITATIVE, QUANTITATIVE INTERFACING

Expertise in the use of jargon is essential if you want to impress other executives. The aim of most corporate jargon is to confuse your enemies and to show your superiors how clever and up-to-date you are. The corporate infighter who waffles on confidently about inspirational dissatisfaction, Phillips curves, limited pleasure-postponing mechanism, and qualitative, quantitative interfacing will always be listened to with respect. He knows something the others don't. Occasionally someone may demand an explanation, but the usual response is to let it pass (no one wants to display ignorance) or to nod in confirmation, which gives the impression that they, too, are familiar with the latest jargon.

A careful study of business magazines should keep you informed of the

currently fashionable buzz-words. But you can easily make up your own. As noted earlier in this book (page 20), the basic principle is never to use a simple word or phrase if you can find a complex one. A garden, for example, should always be called a 'recreational eco-unit', which makes a space a 'manually-operated recreational eco-unit maintenance tool'.

Once you have mastered the art, you should be able to stun your colleagues into awed silence. Throw in, for good measure, a qualifying 'of course' – as in 'of course, if the systemized multiphasic imputation conflicts with the subordinated motivational framework, it may be advisable to utilize the restructured tactical procedure'. It takes courage to challenge that kind of statement. If you *are* challenged, pretend to be horrified that the questioner has not kept in touch with current management thinking and reply with another, equally convoluted sentence.

The game is more difficult if you are playing against another master, who is in a position to expose you. But if you indicate that you may do the same thing to him he will usually leave well alone.

The numbers racket:

The corporate world also pays an extraordinary amount of attention to statistics. We trust them more than we do intelligent argument. Statistics never lie – or so it's said. The reality, of course, is different. Statistics can be made to dance to any tune you want to play. You can put favourable factors in and leave others out. You can adjust, revise, ignore. And you can twist the end product. Successive election campaigns have shown how eminently twistable statistics can be. No one is lying; he is simply interpreting figures in a way favourable to his cause.

A good memory for facts and figures is widely regarded as superior to thought. People have come to accept this to such an extent that you can get away with quoting statistics which are hopelessly out of date and even with inventing your own figures on the spot. Would you believe someone who told you that, out of 40 million left-handed people, 14.8 per cent are likely to marry brunettes or that 68.3 per cent of all barbers are bald? Of course you would. It is the kind of information fed to us by newspapers and magazines all the time. Why should anyone bother to make it up?

Marketing people have added another element: opinion surveys. The public is bombarded with questionnaires – which irritates the busy, cheers the lonely and flatters the insignificant. Who will you vote for? What beer do you like best? What do you think of rhubarb? The answers are reduced to numerical form, cross-analysed by standard categories such as the age, sex and social class of each person interviewed, and then served as a tasty dish. The cheaper surveys frequently make statements based on replies from fewer than fifty people. If half of the male respondents say that they beat their wives twice a week, the businessman who has paid for this useful piece of 'research' will be tempted to conclude that we are a nation of wife-beaters and produce appropriate implements. If half the female respondents say that they are mad about rhubarb, he will assume that there is a vast potential market just waiting for a genius like him.

You can easily procure your own surveys: just ask half a dozen neighbours for their views. The answers will be just as useless, but they should provide impressive backing for whatever pet scheme you are trying to get accepted by your colleagues.

How to make your own jargon

Take any word from the first column, combine it with any from the second column, then add any in the third column.

Total	Organization	Flexibility
Systemized	Monitored	Sapability
Integrated	Management	Options
Parallel	Reciprocal	Mobility
Functional	Digital	Programming
Responsive	Logic	Concept
Optical	Transitional	Time phrases
Compatible	Third generation	Contingency
Balanced	Policy	Decision
Modified	Executive	Preclusions
Subordinated	Multiphasic	Imputation
Restructured	Motivational	Issue
Orchestrated	Tactical	Framework
Horizontal	Qualitative	Procedure
Correlated	Deliberative	Rejection

THE
BATTLE OF
THE SEXES

THE FEMALE INFIGHTER

There is, obviously, a great deal of truth in the familiar argument that women have to work twice as hard to get half as far as men. Despite women's lib, female executives still have trouble breaking into senior management: in a world where men are at the top they remain the outsiders. But hard work and talent are not enough; the female corporate infighter also has to be twice as cunning, twice as good at playing the power game, if she is to overcome the invisible barrier which prevents her from reaching the upper levels of the corporate hierarchy.

Feminists blame it all on blatant sexism and it would clearly be stupid to deny that it exists. Discrimination is a fact of life which no amount of legislation, however well-intentioned, will ever demolish completely. We discriminate against each other all the time and not only on grounds of sex: whites do it to the blacks and vice versa; the rich do it to the poor; Catholics do it to Protestants; Hindus do it to Moslems; countries do it to each other. It is right and proper to complain about prejudice but the intelligent infighter is, or should be, far more concerned with the practical implications. Protest marches may be good for the soul, but you are much more likely to make progress in the corporate world if you take the trouble to find out the reasons for the prejudice against women and resolve to do something about it in your own subtle, clever, scheming way. Don't just attack the 'male chauvinistic pig'; get the better of him.

The worst thing you can do is to put 'The Cause' before your own interests. Leave it to Gloria Steinem and other media people to run the campaign; they are handsomely paid for their articles and TV appearances. *You* cannot afford to take on the male establishment in the same aggressive manner. Men may seem dumb and unjust, but they make the key decisions in large corporations and, like it or not, your career depends on them. Strident demands for 'equality' are invariably counter-productive. They will continue to make concessions, but they will do so in their own good time. Female executives who do battle on behalf of their sex are invariably branded as troublemakers who *have* to be kept in their place. The law may be able to insist on 'equal opportunity', but it cannot force corporations to appoint women to the most important jobs.

Some industries offer more scope for advancement than others – fashion, cosmetics, advertising, publishing, public relations, radio and TV. Financial services such as banking remain deeply conservative – or, if you prefer, reactionary. The initial attitude to women's lib was one of quiet amusement; the brass felt that it could make jokes about it (the movement quickly became known as 'Women's Lip') but that there was no real need for significant concessions. A decade later many managers are prepared to be more flexible – up to a point. There is a greater willingness to acknowledge that women deserve a fair deal, but the same old excuses for keeping them out of the jobs that really matter are still trotted out whenever the subject is discussed in executive dining rooms.

We all know what they are; let us consider how you can counter them.

Women don't take their careers seriously:

The most widely aired argument – based chiefly on the belief that they will eventually leave, either to have children or because the tensions of work become too much. A variation of this is the claim that 'women are not as single-minded as men'. They lack, it is said, the ability to concentrate on business to the exclusion of everything else. It is, of course, a generalization which could just as easily be applied to men. Most people have interests outside work. Some women put their families first; many men regard work as something one has to do between football matches and boozing. Single-mindedness has nothing to do with a person's sex; we all know women who are devoted to their jobs. But it is worth making an effort to show that you *are* serious.

The family question is generally the most difficult to handle and should be met head-on. Make your position absolutely clear. If you already have grown-up children, or are past the child-bearing age, make sure that everyone who counts is aware of the fact.

If you don't intend to have any children, say so and give your reasons.

If you have a young family, go out of your way to prove that it doesn't interfere with your job.

"I'm going to have him for dinner – which wine do you suggest?"

The other issues should also be tackled vigorously. It ought to be relatively easy if you have demonstrated your staying power by years of service, but there is much to be said for reinforcing your case by making it known that you *enjoy* working under pressure and are prepared to take on any task. Make a fuss about your pension rights: it will be seen as further proof that you intend to remain with the corporation for as long as your male colleagues.

Women are not tough enough:

One would have thought that women like Margaret Thatcher and Indira Gandhi had demolished that argument, but it persists. Prove your own gritty toughness from time to time by taking a stand on some matter which you *know* will be resolved in your favour. Tough language is widely regarded as a substitute for action; many men are unable to tell the difference. Study the Thatcher technique and follow her example.

You may also find it useful to take an assertiveness training course. It will teach you (if you need to be taught these things) how to say 'no' when you want to say 'no', 'yes' when you want to say 'yes'; how to speak in a firm voice rather than in a wishy-washy whisper; how to respond to put-downs and so on.

Women are too emotional:

Usually said by men who get upset by the most trivial detail, and who regularly lose their temper. Easily countered by controlling your own temper, whatever the provocation. Tears should be avoided at all cost; if

you feel in need of a good cry, do it at home.

Women don't like taking risks:

Nor do most men; you either have courage or you don't. Go after high-risk, high-reward line positions. That is what Mrs Thatcher did when her male colleagues were reluctant to have a go.

Men don't want to do business with women:

Rubbish. They will do business with *anyone* if they think it is to their advantage. Prove it by doing a profitable deal and making sure that you get the credit.

Women demand special treatment:

Some do: they assume that they merit extra consideration *because* they are women. Their male rivals find this irritating and one can hardly blame them. Make it plain that you expect to be treated just like a man – that you have no intention of

demanding special favours. You don't have to refuse small courtesies, like having a door help opened for you, but you should not take them for granted either.

One of the silliest excuses for not promoting women is that there are no separate toilet facilities on the management floor. This generally turns out to be quite untrue, but you may still come across it. Tell them that you have no objection to sharing their washroom with them. They will be shocked, of course, but it is a good way of showing just how ridiculous the argument is.

Men don't feel comfortable with women:

What this means usually is that they can't swear or tell dirty jokes in their presence. They feel that if they use bad language in the heat of debate they have to apologize. One obvious answer is to swear yourself and to have your own store of dubious jokes. But there really is no need to do so: it is enough to assure them that your ears are not *that* delicate.

Assets

The cards may be stacked against the female corporate infighter, but she *does* have advantages which can and should be exploited.

One is that, in power struggles, men consistently underrate women. Male chauvinist pride being what it is, they find it difficult to see them as dangerous rivals. Most of their warfare is directed at other men; they simply cannot believe that they might be defeated by the 'weaker sex'. By the time they realize that a women has, after all, managed to get the better of them, it is usually too late to do anything about it.

Another plus, closely linked, is that men are much more inclined to share confidences with women than with male colleagues. They want to impress them and, because they do not regard females as a serious threat, they talk frankly about their clever schemes and ambitious plans. Their vanity makes them assumes that you are automatically on their side and it is a simple matter to get them to reveal everything you need to know: all you have to do is to give them a little encouragement.

This arrogant belief in the natural superiority of the male can be exploited in other ways. Most men are, for example, eager to offer advice. Let them do so, even if you already know the answers: they will let you know more about themselves in a few minutes than you can get in a month of observation, and if you subsequently appear to be acting on it they will feel duty bound to support you. Don't complain about 'paternalism', however irritating it may be. View it as a source of ammunition.

HUSBANDS

Husbands can be a nuisance, which is why so many female corporate infighters prefer to stay single. They marry their jobs and use their subordinates (and projects) as offspring.

Women's magazines are always full of comforting comments. 'If you made it clear that your job is important to you when you got married,' they say, 'your husband can't object if you go on doing so.' Unfortunately, a lot of them do. The male view that wives should stay at home and take care of the domestic chores, instead of going after the chief executive's job, still has a far greater hold than feminists would like. Some men don't mind reversing the traditional roles: the 'house-husband' is no longer a rarity. But the majority find it hard to accept that a woman's place is in the office.

"My boss, Mrs. Rankin, will be there, so put on loads of that sexy after-shave of yours."

Those who don't object often get tetchy if the job becomes too demanding. They welcome the money, but they don't want to take second place. If their wives are more successful than they are, there is also a risk that they will become envious, especially if both partners work in the same line of business.

This, clearly, is a problem which every career woman has to solve in whatever manner seems most appropriate. You may be blessed with an understanding and supportive mate, but it pays to bear some basic points in mind.

Men need reassurance:

So do women, but we are talking about husbands. Make sure that he doesn't feel neglected. A woman who puts her career first at all times can upset even the most understanding mate. Be flexible.

Don't compete:

Compete with your rivals in the office, not with the man in your life. It may be gratifying to outdo him, but don't rub it in. It will undermine his self-confidence and embarrass him. Play down your achievements and praise his.

Get domestic help:

Sharing housework with your husband may seem like a good idea, but most men do it with great reluctance. If you have to cope with the office *and* the home you are bound to get irritable and rows inevitably follow. Let someone else take care of the chores; the expenditure is well worthwhile.

Avoid long business trips:

Absence doesn't *always* make the heart grow fonder. It can just as easily lead to alienation. If you are frequently away he may look for solace elsewhere. (The same, of course, also applies to women.) Avoid boozy conventions – they are generally a waste of time anyway.

Stress the advantages:

He knows about the money, but he may not always appreciate the other pluses. A wife who has a satisfying career is more interesting than one who doesn't. (She has much more to talk about.) She is also more likely to maintain her appearance and she is able to make new friends which both of you can share. If she holds an influential position, she may be able to help her husband in all kinds of ways: she can certainly give informed advice.

If none of this works – if he insists that you abandon your career – divorce the brute. He isn't the only man in the world.

HOW TO DRESS FOR SUCCESS

If you don't want to be viewed as a sex object, don't dress like one. If you turn up at the office in a short, tight-fitting leather skirt and a blouse slashed to the naval, or dripping with lace, your male colleagues will find it hard to keep their minds on balance sheets.

Male executives are expected to make their appearance coincide with the company's image (see page 80). Female executives should do the same. In the so-called glamour industries such as fashion, cosmetics, advertising and public relations, women are expected to show flair and individuality in their clothes; in more conservative fields, such as banking, they are required to look businesslike, but not aggressive, dull or dowdy.

If you work for a large corporation, a tailored suit (with a skirt rather than trousers) is generally best. It gives you that essential air of authority. Add an attractive silk blouse or shirt – and yes, it's all right to wear the company tie if everyone else is doing the same.

Avoid anything that is too extreme – flamboyant hats (men tend to find them ridiculous), elaborate and expensive jewellery (you want people to talk about your business talents, not about your collection of baubles) and mink coats. (They will naturally wonder how you can afford one on your salary.)

An executive briefcase is preferable to a handbag. The contents may be the same, but it will enhance your businesslike appearance. If you must carry a handbag, it should be of natural leather and as small and unobtrusive as possible.

Go easy on the scent – you don't want to risk male complaints that the meetings you attend smell like a boudoir.

Keep your hair short and neat (as male executives do) but avoid hair-styles which make you look like a tough school-mistress.

The aim, at all times, must be to look cool, professional, elegant, quietly efficient. What you wear outside the office is your affair; what you wear in the office is the company's business as well as yours and will certainly affect your career.

THE OTHER WOMAN

It would seem reasonable to assume, after all the fuss about women's lib, that female corporate infighters who *have* made it to the top are eager to help others to achieve the same kind of breakthrough. No doubt some are, but it's unwise to count on it.

The awkward truth is that battle-hardened women are primarily concerned with looking after Number One. They feel, or seem to feel, that others should go through the same tough process and don't want to be burdened with the responsibilities that go with patronage. Some actually take pleasure in making things difficult. Perhaps they think that another woman's success would detract from their own achievement, or perhaps they simply enjoy wielding power and find it easier to bully men than women. It may even be that, in the long climb to the upper reaches of the corporate hierarchy, they have adopted some of the prejudices they used to condemn. Whatever the reason, many ambitious young women have made the upsetting discovery that a female boss is often harder to deal with than a male chauvinist.

Don't be misled by the smile on her face: there is absolutely no guarantee that she will be a friend. It is much more likely that she will see you as a potential rival and use all the formidable skills acquired in years of struggle to ensure that you are kept in your place. If you are younger and better-looking (and therefore more likely to attract male flattery), she will resent it. If you have talent and drive, she will be suspicious. If *her* superior singles you out for praise, she will be furious.

You *may* be lucky enough to find a female boss whose reactions are very different – who is kind, generous, understanding, supportive. She will probably be someone who has given up all hope of rising any higher and therefore sees no point in being bitchy. But it is clearly naive to assume that all women are comrades standing shoulder to shoulder against an army of ruthless men. Some of those 'comrades' will happily shoot you in the back.

If you *are* working for one of these Amazons, be on your guard. Don't say anything which might be used against you. Ignore her ups and downs. Be polite; never show that her criticism or current put-down has reached you. Don't try to upstage her. Behave towards her just as you would towards anyone else in the corporation; forget the fact that she is a woman. She is an executive who has won many battles and intends to win more. Try to persuade her that she has nothing to fear – and then be sure to shoot first.

SEX IN THE OFFICE

The women's magazine are right: sex should be kept *out* of the office. There are so many opportunities elsewhere that you really have no excuse for dallying on the premises, in the company's time. This is certainly the view taken by the brass, who tend to be hard on people who insist on disrupting the proceedings in such a frivolous way. Many promising careers have been wrecked by sexual gamesmanship.

But, of course, sex is *not* kept out of offices. Not all of them, anyway. There are always people who regard them as convenient playgrounds. They take chances because they think that they are clever enough not to be found out; some actually enjoy the element of danger. Boredom, ego gratification and the inability (or unwillingness) to resist a tempting opportunity lead many executives to embark on liaisons which, more often than not, they subsequently regret.

Sometimes they end in marriage – even bosses have been known to marry their secretaries – but affairs are much more common. They vary from casual 'sex is fun' adventures to passionate and, while they last, serious and demanding relationships.

Men generally get the blame and probably deserve it, but women are not always the hapless victims of crafty and persuasive male predators. They often take the initiative themselves, either because they are on the look-out for potential husbands or because they think that an affair with an influential executive will help to secure promotion.

Can you sleep your way to the top? It *has* been done (notably in Hollywood) but it is a risky strategy. No matter what exalted position a besotted lover may put you in, you can only stay there with talent and brains. If you lack the ability to do well in a responsible post you will, sooner or later, be down-graded or fired. A lover can help you up the corporate ladder, and give you useful protection, but he can't do the job for you.

The problem with affairs, casual or otherwise, is that they seldom *do* remain a secret, even if you take basic precautions such as continuing to use Mr and Miss (or Mrs) in the office, going to work separately, though you live together, and not confiding your love to anyone you work with. There are so many tell-tale signs which give you away: the exchange of intimate glances (invariably

noticed by others present), the natural tendency to support each other in every situation, the frequent lunches together in the office dining room or in nearby restaurants, the personal phone calls and so on. Once your relationship has been discovered, word will get around very quickly. People like to gossip and many have a vested interest in bringing the relationship to the attention of your superiors. If they see that you get preferential treatment because of your affair, they will naturally resent it. There may also be jealous colleagues who have had their own advances rebuffed and are determined to get their revenge.

The other problem is that all kinds of unpleasant things tend to happen when the sweet talk turns sour. The once-so-helpful lover can turn into a vicious brute. He suddenly recognizes that it was all a ghastly mistake and charges off in the opposite direction. He makes life as difficult for you as he can and may even try to rid himself of your embarrassing presence. If you dally with someone else he is liable to become even nastier. People are very possessive about their sexual conquests and don't like to see someone else getting something they no longer have – even when they're done with it.

Discarded mistresses can be just as malevolent. You may recall the case of the well-known US Congressman who discarded his secretary/mistress after a prolonged affair and married *another* secretary. His former lover (whose salary had been paid out of public funds) decided to give the story to the press and the scandal made headlines for weeks. Then there was the equally famous case of the British Minister, Cecil Parkinson, who made his secretary pregnant, promised to marry her and then went back to his wife. The rejected mistress also decided to tell the newspapers about it and the Minister felt compelled to resign his high office.

The lesson is obvious: don't mess around at work, especially not with your secretary. Even if you are the head of a department, or a member of the Board, you can run into trouble. Your subordinates will find a way of telling your colleagues – and, perhaps worse, your wife – about the affair. You will be laughed at behind your back and colleagues will express doubts about your judgement.

Affairs out of the office tend to receive much greater tolerance. The general view is that you are entitled to do what you like in your own time, providing it doesn't interfere with your job. A liaison with someone who works for a rival corporation may even be regarded as helpful; pillow talk can be a useful ally if one is interested in industrial espionage. Companies have been known to engage good-looking young men and women for just this purpose.

SEXUAL HARASSMENT

However determind you are to avoid office entanglements you may, at times, be subjected to what is fashionably know as sexual harassment. If you are young and attractive it may happen quite often.

Unwanted advances can be extremely annoying and rightly infuriate the feminists. Their stock advice is to reject them vigorously and, if necessary, to report the offender to his superiors or even to take legal action.

But an angry response, however justified, may harm your career (especially if the offender is your boss) and it is generally better to try to resolve the problem by other means. A firm but polite rebuff may do the trick, and leave the relationship intact. If it doesn't, you can still resort to tougher methods.

Many men are really cowards; they feel that they ought to have a go but are really relieved when they are turned down. (They tend to fall back on some lame remark like: 'I'm glad you did that; I was just testing you.') A once-only proposition does not amount to harassment, and it is unwise to react too strongly. Don't make threats unless, and until, you feel that you have no alternative. Don't go out of your way to make unnecessary enemies.

A wedding ring is a mute signal to keep away; if you don't want to be propositioned by *anyone* in the office wear one, even if you are unmarried. If it turns out to be an inadequate defence, try one or more of these lines:

I am flattered, but my husband/fiancé wouldn't approve.

Have you seen these pictures of my kids?

I like this job, and I wouldn't want to put it at risk.

Thank you, but it would make it impossible to work together.

I really can't cope with my job *and* an emotional involvement.

It's nothing personal; I just don't go out with married men.

Come now, you *know* how the company feels about these things. Don't jeopardize your career as well as mine.

It helps, of couse, to know the different types of predators and their techniques. Here are some of the common species:

The Don Juan:

The Don Juan is an experienced (and often disturbingly attractive) philanderer with an extensive repertoire of ploys which have served him well in the past. He knows how to flatter and he promises to be discreet. He can be great fun, but he is also the type of man who is most likely to drop his mistress after making her neglect her work and making her the focus of spiteful gossip by colleagues who have seen it all before.

The Ambitious Rival:

He – or she – deliberately uses sex as a weapon in the office war. The primary aim is to turn you into an obedient slave, but there are often other reasons. He – or she – may seek to expose your weakness and remove you from competition.

The Amorous Boss:

The Amorous Boss assumes that female subordinates are among his perks, and that a career woman will recognize – and use – his influence. He is often quite open about this: he will take her to lunch and put his case as bluntly as if he were negotiating a business deal. He may or may not deliver; if he thinks that promoting her cause is not to his advantage he will probably keep making promises but never actually *do* anything.

If your boss makes an overt pass at you, and it is unwelcome, take it seriously and calmly, no matter how annoyed you may be. Point out that a

"I firmly believe that one shouldn't have an affaire with anyone working within the same organisation as oneself. Elspeth, would you mind terribly finding employment elsewhere?"

sexual relationship would make it impossible to work efficiently together. Don't make him feel that you are rejecting him because you find him unattractive and don't make fun of him; make sure that your reasons are quite impersonal. Remind him that many such liaisons damage the careers of both parties, and that you respect him too much to risk spoiling what could, and should, be a productive partnership. He will usually accept that your argument makes sense; if he doesn't, try to seek a transfer to another department or, if that fails, apply for a job with another company.

The Husband-Hunter:

This kind of predator is much more common than feminists seem prepared to acknowledge: her principal ambition is to ensnare a man whose career is more likely to prosper than her own. She makes every effort to show that she would be a loyal and supportive wife who, having worked for the same company, would understand his aims and problems and help him to reach the top. She is not deterred by the fact that her quarry may already be married; she knows that the divorce rate among corporation men is higher than it has ever been before.

Many such women *do* make excellent wives. But they can be very nasty if one rejects them and it pays to be cautious.

The Office Lecher:

He will chase *anything* in skirts: his mind is always on sex and he operates on the principle that, if you proposition ten women, six may slap your face but one or two may well say 'yes'. His conversation is full of sexual innuendo and he likes to tell dirty jokes just to see what reaction he gets. He says things like 'Let me show you what I learned from the *Kama Sutra*' and 'What are you saving it for?' The Office Lecher will probably take 'no' for an answer, and try his luck elsewhere, but he may also persist. Sexual harassment is his speciality. Never give him the slightest encouragement, intentionally or otherwise, and make it clear that, if he continues to be obnoxious, you will not hesitate to report him.

The Romantic:

The Romantic falls in love easily and often. He leaves ardent messages on your desk (where everyone can read them), calls six times a day, sends flowers and hangs around the office like a faithful puppy-dog. His devoted attention can be an awful nuisance and he is generally hard to shake off. If you take pity on him he will be pathetically grateful – until he falls in love with one of the other girls.

. The Romantic is dangerous because he is good at exploiting the emotions of others and because he makes such a big performance out of his temporary attachments. It is usually best to make it absolutely plain, right from the start, that he is wasting his time.

The Story-Teller:

The Story-Teller loves to bore others with accounts of his sexual conquests, most of which never actually happened. 'This secretary was crazy about me . . . she would do anything, absolutely anything . . . couldn't keep her hands off me.' Or 'this executive over at X corporation, very bright and attractive, asked me to dinner and then took me back to her apartment. Oh, boy! Now, of course, she calls me every day.' His aim is to impress and intrigue you; he hopes that you will want to find out for yourself what makes him so irresistible. Don't bother; remember that, if you give him the slightest encouragement, his next tale will be about *you*. 'This executive in the marketing department . . . '

"You are ideally qualified to be chief executive of this company but I'm afraid the men here are already under too much stress!"

Away Games

People who normally behave with great propriety in the office often become different personalities when they go on business trips or attend conventions. They seem hell-bent on making up for lost time.

Don't imagine that distance guarantees safety: *someone* will always notice and is quite likely to tell others about it. The office sneak who discovers that a rival is making a fool of himself has acquired a useful weapon. He may or may not use it; sometimes he settles for a little blackmail.

If you must indulge in bedroom frolics away from base, choose a partner who has no connection with the company. Male executives should leave their secretaries at home; it wouldn't be hard to find another playmate. Female executives should try to ward off the boozy attention of colleagues who think that at convention anything goes; you can't embark on an intimate relationship and expect the other person to behave as if nothing has happened when you get back.

FAMILY
MATTERS

THE CORPORATE WIFE

Anne regards herself as the perfect corporate wife. She doesn't believe in Women's Lib – indeed, she makes a point of reassuring men that, in her view, it is all a lot of nonsense. Libbers treat her with contempt, but she reckons that her interests are better served by a traditional attitude. Her husband's career comes first. It doesn't mean that she lacks ambition – she is more ambitious than he is – but she feels that in a male-dominated business world her chances of material progress are greater if she helps *him* to 'get on'.

'Good corporate wives' like Anne come from middle-class backgrounds and accept the system. If they have working-class origins they try to disguise them. It may mean discarding childhood friends but this is a price they gladly pay. They dress well (but not too sexily) and look after neat suburban homes. They don't complain when their husbands have to work long hours, or are sent abroad on business trips. In short, they are everything that corporations expect the wives of their rising executives to be.

Many corporations try to find out as much as possible about the wives of job candidates. Will she be understanding and totally supportive of the man as he takes on his demanding responsibilities? Will she be a social asset? The assessment is made subtly and surreptitiously, but it is often a key factor. And, of course, the surveillance continues for years to come.

Anne knows this and does her best to show her husband's bosses that she is part of the corporate team. But it is all a show: deep down, she hates the corporation and what it is doing to their home life. It robs her of his time and is a rival for his affection. He comes home late, worried and irritable, and either makes straight for the television set or retreats into his study to do more paper work. Dinner is eaten in silence – or, if he has had a particularly annoying

118

day, she has to listen to a long tirade against all the people in the office who insist on making his life so difficult. She would like to talk about *her* problems – the stultifying boredom, the impossible behaviour of the children, the unpaid bills – but she doesn't want him to be more depressed than he is already.

Her sex life is unsatisfactory: he is always too tired (nowadays it is the husband who tends to get headaches) and she has resigned herself to making do with a perfunctory Saturday night performance. She has considered having an affair, but is terrified of losing her meal ticket. She reads a lot of sexy novels and magazines like *Cosmopolitan* but misses the romance of their courting days.

They often quarrel about money. She runs the family budget and resents the fact that he doesn't seem to understand inflation. She has no savings of her own so she has to ask him for everything, which invariably leads to arguments. 'If he had to pay for all I do,' she complains to friends, 'it would cost him a small fortune.' She thinks that his salary ought to be higher than it is and frequently urges him to ask for a rise, or for promotion. Despite her public display of loyalty to the corporation, she would be quite happy if he took another job with a bigger income.

From time to time they talk about 'getting out of the rat race'. He talks enthusiastically about buying a farm or a restaurant in that marvellous little resort they went to last summer. She lets him dream, and is half-inclined to agree, but her instincts tell her to be cautious: what if the venture fails? Is he really up to it? Could he get another job if they get into financial trouble? Better the devil you know. . . .

Corporate wives whose husbands are doing well – whose careers are progressing nicely – at least have the satisfaction of being able to count on a rising income. An intelligent woman who is married to someone who is getting nowhere, no matter how hard he tries, is in a much worse position. One of the most difficult moments in her life is when she is forced to recognize that all the exciting talk of wealth and power is likely to remain just that – talk. She desperately wants him to 'get on', and rarely misses a chance to promote his cause, but she cannot do his job for him. She lives in constant fear that he will come home one day and tell her that he has been fired. She may have complained for years that he is not devoting enough time to the family but the prospect of having him around all the time is horrifying.

Some corporate wives are alcoholics; some divorce their husbands and marry men who appear to be more dynamic. (Men, too, are much more ready nowadays to discard wives who cannot keep pace. One divorce is generally acceptable; two or more may be looked at askance.)

Most wives, though, manage to hide their discontent from the people who are in a position to shape their men's careers. They strive to present a helpful picture of domestic stability and often exercise considerable power behind the scenes. A Harris poll conducted on behalf of *Business Week* showed that wives have a big say in career choices – whether, and where, to take an assignment – and in matters such as the timing of retirement. Some sixty-two per cent of the male executives questioned by the pollsters even admitted that their wives were influential to some degree in the decision where to site the corporate headquarters. They also conceded – Women's Libbers, please note – that they influence the hiring of women. Just over fifty-five per cent said that they were

119

"I'm not quite sure how to put this darling, but ever since we've had the house modernised you don't fit in any more."

swayed by the opinions of their wives.

Wives know how feeble men can be when faced by an attractive and intelligent career woman, and they are usually good at protecting their interests. To them, such women (especially those who are single) represent a threat and they generally know how to deal with them. A common ploy is to invite the potential rival to a cocktail party, or dinner, for an on-the-spot assessment. If she is elderly and ugly, there is no problem. If not, the defensive mechanism moves into high gear. Her faults are carefully analysed and brought to the husband's attention in a dozen subtle ways. He – naive boy! – may not even be aware that the advice he gets is not unbiased.

Men tend to have an easier run, *unless* they are perceived to be rival candidates for a job which wives have earmarked for their husbands. Armed with female intuition, and free from the burden of office friendships, they are quick to spot a weakness and husbands are urged to make the most of it: every shared confidence, every careless remark is seen as a useful weapon.

As the corporate infighter advances in rank his wife, too, gains increasing power. A quiet word from her can make or break a subordinate's career. Everyone in corporate life knows how useful it is to have the support of the woman who is married to the chairman or chief executive. The best way to secure it is to listen to what she has to say and agree with every word, even if she is talking rubbish.

When years of relentless pressure finally catches up with the husband, and he has a fatal heart attack, the corporate wife collects the insurance money and, in many cases, turns into a merry widow. You can see her on Caribbean cruises – she is the one with the blue rinse, Yves St Laurent dress and diamond necklace. During the husband's lifetime she played the role of a dutiful wife; now she eagerly tries to be the *femme fatale* she always wanted to be. She gives parties and flirts with any reasonably good-looking male who catches her eye. Her frantic efforts to make up for lost time often strike others as rather pathetic, but few have the courage to say so in her presence.

Keeping the corporate wife happy while the infighter pursues his career objectives is clearly not an easy task. But every effort should be made to preserve a helpful front. Wives should be carefully trained in the art of corporate warfare and kept in touch with day-to-day developments. It makes them feel involved and prevents embarrassing behaviour.

Japanese women are said to make the best corporate wives in the world; liberated American women are reputedly the worst. But such generalizations don't mean very much: it is up to the infighter to ensure that his wife is an asset rather than a liability.

Basic rules for corporate wives:

Never push your husband beyond his capabilities. When it becomes painfully apparent that he is not up to the job, humiliation follows.

Never prod him into a confrontation he cannot win. Listen to his grievances and sympathize, but be utterly realistic about his chances of success.

Never promote his cause with excessive enthusiasm; a lot of senior corporation men are irritated by wives who are 'too pushy' and you may actually be doing him harm if you use social occasions to tell them how good he is.

Never challenge his statements, or argue with his opinions, if anyone else from the corporation is present, even if you know that he is telling lies. It is not your job to expose him.

Never tell the wives of his colleagues or superiors anything which might conceivably be used against him, even if they appear to be good friends. Keep your pillow talk to yourself. Don't tell them what he really thinks of the brass, and under no circumstances reveal his doubts and worries.

Never try to upstage the wives of his superiors at company cocktail parties and dinners. They will be furious and will almost certainly retaliate by making disparaging remarks about you – and him – to their own husbands.

Never complain to his superiors about the demands they make on his time and energies; it will make them wonder about his ability to take on the even greater workload which goes with promotion.

Never embarrass him by criticizing aspects of company policy, or expressing views which might conceivably be regarded as 'left-wing'.

Never press your husband to take on financial commitments he can't handle; executives who have money worries find it hard to concentrate on their work and, worse, may make foolish moves – such as taking another job simply because it means a little more cash.

Never make an enemy out of his secretary: she should be your closest ally.

THE CORPORATE HOME

The corporate infighter's home *should* be his private domain – a place where he can relax after a hard day in the office or do battle with his family. But, of course, there are times when he may find it expedient to invite his boss, colleagues or business contacts for cocktails, dinner or weekend meetings. As he climbs up the corporate ladder it becomes more and more likely that others will get a glimpse of his domestic life-style. People will certainly talk about it – one cannot prevent them from doing so. It clearly matters that their comments should be flattering.

Suburbia is made in corporation man's imagine: all those neat houses and gardens, oozing middle-class respectability, augment the picture he is trying to present to the world. Some corporations have taken this to its logical conclusion and created company towns. They tend to be rather like army settlements, with the same kind of clearly defined social structure. The inhabitants may be allowed somewhat greater freedom to express their individuality, but it is dangerous to step too far out of line. The man who insists on painting his house yellow, when every other house in the street is white, runs the risk that people will question his ability to function as a member of the team.

Company towns, it is claimed, strengthen the employee's sense of belonging and give corporations greater scope for looking after their own. They have their own shopping centres, schools and even hospitals. It sounds good in theory; in practice they amount to an effort to control his whole life. Stay clear of them if you possibly can.

Because his home is a status symbol, a measure of his success, the corporate executive wil naturally do his best to find one which will properly reflect whatever position he has attained. He would, of course, like it to be comfortable, but this is not as important as having the 'right home' in the 'right area'. If he was born and raised in a working-class district he will generally want to move out at the earliest opportunity, even though it means taking on heavy financial commitments. It's not just a matter of advertising one's success; he also knows that his superiors will think less of him if he continues to live among his old friends (most of whom probably belong to one of those troublesome trade unions) in his old neighbourhood. He will be marked down as a man who does not understand the importance of upward mobility.

A detached house has more status than a semi-detached; a large garden is more impressive than a small one. But it is considered bad form to buy a home in the same street as the chief executive, and under no circumstances should

you upstage him by looking for one which is bigger or smarter than his. He will be furious and your prospects of promotion will be sharply reduced, not only because he will want to punish you for your presumptuousness but also because he will not want anyone to think that he favoured you because you are a close neighbour. A likely response is a request that you should be transferred to a division in another town, and of course that is exactly what will happen. You will not be told the real reason; the usual tactic is to tell the executive that he must 'broaden his experience' or that his particular type of expertise is urgently needed elsewhere.

Inside, most corporate homes have standard features like three-piece suites, cocktail cabinets and pine kitchens. But you *may* be invited to visit one of the top men's homes and it's useful to have some idea what they will look like.

The chairman's house:

The chairman of a large corporation is expected to live in a rambling country house, somewhere near a golf course. (An estate is better; it allows him to play the part-time role of gentleman farmer.) It should have a library with lots of leather-bound books, even if he never gets around to reading any of them. The dining room should be huge, with expensive wood panelling. There should be a rose garden and, of course, the lawn should be in impeccable condition. Riding stables and a heated swimming pool are optional extras. A tennis court is a *must*; he may not use it, but it will be appreciated by the more energetic members of the family and by visitors, including important overseas business contacts, who come for the weekend. (The head of one major British corporation plays what one of his friends calls 'chairman's tennis'. He stands at the centre of the court and waits for the ball to come to him; running after it, he clearly feels, is undignified for a man in his august position. Subordinates complain that it makes it very difficult for them to lose.) There should be at least three servants – a maid, a gardener and a chauffeur – and the family pet should be a bulldog or a St Bernard.

Corporate infighters who are invited to the chairman's home should praise the roses, the cooking and his port. Gushing comments on the house itself should be avoided, unless he is one of those *nouveaux riches* businessmen who still can't get over the fact that they have done so much better than anyone expected. It is essential to make sure that one is liked by the dog; many chairmen have more faith in the judgement of their dogs than they have in their own.

The chief executive's home office:

If the chairman is also the chief executive, and the head office is some distance away from his country home, he will probably spend weekdays in his town house or luxury apartment. This enables him to go on working until late at night, or to put in an appearance at some of the numerous functions to which he is invited. Senior executives will be summoned to working sessions after hours, and left to make their own way home to the suburbs when he decides to let them go. He will graciously offer them a drink or two, and sometimes dinner is provided, but these are *not* social occasions and it is unwise to relax too much. Don't look at your watch, and go easy on the gin. Some bosses regard working sessions as a splendid opportunity to deliver long monologues, rather like Hitler's Table Talk. Don't interrupt, even if you are desperately worried about catching the last train.

Young, energetic and ambitious chief executives are particularly inclined to treat town residences as an extension of their offices. The obligatory study is equipped with push-botton telephones and a desk computer (so that he can check up on the latest sales and production figures) and there will usually be a video machine, so that he can watch his latest pep talk before it is sent out to the divisions.

If he is married, and his wife and children are around, they will usually be kept out of the way. Work is considered more important. The wife will be expected to look after the domestic arrangemets, and may be introduced to subordinates, but she will not take part in the discussions. The children are supposed to be busy doing their homework, but they will almost certainly be watching television: he will be too busy to notice. It does not, as a rule, matter what they do as long as they don't clutter up the place with bicycles and other playthings: the one thing he can't stand is an untidy home.

The marketing director's showcase:

The marketing director's home may come as a surprise: people who move in this curious world (see page 19) often feel compelled to demonstrate that they are creative types and can therefore afford to be more adventurous than other corporation men. Marketing and advertising people tend to choose homes which they hope will make them look trendy, and to fill them with eye-catching but uncomfortable furniture: gleaming steel chairs, bright red or yellow sofas, acrylic side tables and lamps which resemble spaceships about to take off for Mars. The walls may feature those awful Andy Warhol paintings of beer cans and frankfurters with ketchup, though Warhol is nowadays regarded as rather old-fashioned and has probably been replaced by one of those weird pseudo-geniuses who seem to be obsessed with giant breasts and penises. It is all showmanship: at weekends they slink off, gratefully, to some cosy old-fashioned cottage in the country.

The finance director's house:

Finance directors are conservative people and this is generally reflected in the way they live. They have a penchant for Victorian and mock-Tudor houses, and the interiors tend to be functional rather than imaginative. Some contain valuable antiques, and you will probably be told that they represent a good investment. Everything will be neat and tidy: finance directors like order and their wives have been trained accordingly. (They also, of course, keep a tight grip on household budgets and you are unlikely to be offered more than a small glass of sherry.) There will probably be a vase filled with plastic flowers – they are cheaper – and you may find a chess set on the coffee table, next to old copies of the *Economist*. Remember to wipe your feet as you go in, and for goodness sake don't spill any ash on the carpet.

The production director's gadgets:

The production director is a great believer in domestic gadgets; he is all for improving efficiency in the home as well as in the factory. He talks enthusiastically about the time – not far off, he thinks – when all the housework will be done by robots. His wife has mixed feelings about all this: she does not object to labour-saving devices but hates to see her cosy nest turned into an automated plant and is very much aware that, if any of the gadgets should go wrong, she will be the one who has to get them repaired. He has, however, been allowed to convert his study into a 'home work station' complete with computer, word processor and a micro-electronic private branch exchange. He likes nothing better than to disappear into the station before and after dinner and play with his toys. He also applies modern production methods to gardening; he proudly points out that his tomatoes and cucumbers are the biggest in the neighbourhood.

Visitors would be well advised to express admiration for his bag of tricks and to listen patiently to his lecture on what the home of tomorrow *ought* to look like. It may strike you as appallingly soulless, but don't let him think that you are one of those old-fashioned people who resist what he regards as progress.

The Corporate Home
Assets
Lampshades made from old
   share certificates
Bonsai trees
Copies of *Vogue*
Japanese screens
Persian carpets
Home computers
Marble bath
Golf clubs, riding hats, tennis
   rackets
Books by P.G. Wodehouse
Hunting prints
Sauna
Silver candlesticks
Four-poster beds
Regency wine coasters
Silk cushions
Framed paintings by the children
Piano
Framed photos of corporate

social occasions (they help to
   prove loyalty to the
   corporation)

Liabilities
Garden gnomes
Plastic flowers
Gilded reproduction furniture
Cuckoo clocks
Cheap holiday souvenirs:
   Mexican hats, Spanish dolls,
   German beer mugs
Books by Harold Robbins
Copies of *Playboy*
Electric log fires
Net curtains
Set of flying ducks over the
   fireplace
Door chimes playing a Bing
   Crosby tune or, worse, the
   National Anthem
Mickey Mouse telephone

A home with a name has more status than one which is merely numbered, and care should be taken to choose the right one. How will it look on your personal letterhead? Avoid the obvious, but also beware of the pretentious. Foreign names are all right – they show that you have travelled – but make sure you understand what they mean before you order that brass plate. Never call a house 'Shangri-La' or 'Chez Nous'; if you buy one which already has one of those vulgar labels, change it at once. Some corporate infighters try to show their loyalty to the company by choosing names associated with its activities – a successful advertising slogan, perhaps, or a product which has done well. It can be helpful, but one tends to look a bit stupid when one changes jobs.

ENTERTAINING AT HOME

The food is not all that important, unless you happen to be entertaining a visitor from France. One is generally safe with steak, duck or chicken. If you serve anything fancy, like caviar, you will be regarded as a pretentious show-off and/or as a spendthrift who cannot be trusted with an expense account, let alone a departmental budget. Wines should be French, not Californian, and they should be in the middle-price range. It is bad form to serve some of the ghastly cheap stuff they nowadays sell in off licences, but equally wrong to choose a wine which everyone knows is outrageously expensive. There is nothing more boring than the wine snob who not only insists on making an elaborate performance out of the whole business but is also crass enough to tell his guests how much he paid for each bottle.

If your boss and his wife are coming to dinner for the first time, resist the temptation to invite anyone else. Give the two wives a chance to get to know each other. For other occasions the guest list should be compiled with meticulous care. You will naturally have the good sense to avoid trade union

militants and other left-wing agitators, but you should also beware of less obvious troublemakers like ardent feminists, who tend to irritate everyone with their passionate denouncement of docile corporate wives and biased male employers. Here is a brief guide to the kind of people who can usually be relied on to enhance your prestige:

A Lord:

Peers of the realm don't count for as much as they would like to think, but like French counts and Italian princes they still tend to make impressive dinner guests. Make sure, though, that you don't get saddled with one of those uncouth life peers who used to be a big wheel in the trade union movement and enjoys telling long anecdotes about his battles with the bosses.

An MP:

They tend to lecture others on fiscal policy and industrial management, even though most of them couldn't run a hot dog stand, let alone a MacDonalds franchise. They like to give the impression that they are deeply involved in the process of governing. This, of course, is not so, but businessmen tend to listen to them with interest and wives are usually delighted with their 'inside' stories (which they have probably read in the newspapers) about the Prime Minister, the Foreign Secretary and other luminaries. Play safe by sticking to Tories.

A civil servant:

Senior civil servants really are involved in governing, and if you can land a Permanent Secretary (they tend to be elusive creatures) your reputation will get an enormous boost. Under no circumstances, though, should you invite anyone who is connected with the Inland Revenue: your other guests will, not unreasonably, suspect that he will try to trap them into revealing their favourite tax fiddles.

A banker:

Bankers make amiable dinner companions, and having one among your guests helps to establish that you have useful connections outside the corporation. They are naturally cautious, so you don't have to fear that they will say anything controversial.

A doctor:

Doctors, especially surgeons, tend to talk mostly about their work, but most people find it fascinating and, of course, it is useful to have someone on the spot if one of the other guests chokes on a fishbone or has a heart attack between the soup and the main course.

Doctors are often asked for free advice on various ailments and some get very annoyed by these attempts to exploit social occasions. There is a story about a general practitioner who the next morning sent his fellow guest, a businessman, a bill. A few days later the businessman found himself sitting next to a lawyer at another dinner party. He told him about the doctor's move and asked: 'Can he do that?' The lawyer said 'yes' – and the next morning *he* sent him a bill. Try to forestall trouble by gently but firmly steering such people towards guests (such as the aforementioned MP) who are more than happy to give free advice on all and everything.

A television personality:

TV personalities usually have only one topic of conversation: themselves. But most people like to see what they look like in the flesh and they are generally quite amusing. If they are actors or actresses they tend to be a bit lost without a script but they always make an effort: the dining room is just another stage or television studio. They will call everyone 'darling' but your boss is unlikely to object; it is, after all, what one expects from such people. Praise them as much as you can if you want them back for another engagement; they can absorb any amount of flattery.

HOW TO MAKE SMALL TALK

It is always best to let others do the talking at a company function. Few executives can resist the temptation to impress an attractive woman with tales of their exploits – and you may learn something which can be used to your husband's advantage. If you are introduced to a top man, or find yourself sitting next to him at dinner, you may feel the urge to yawn as he prattles on about the stock market, economic indices, interest rates and product development. Suppress it. To him, they are the most important topics in the world. Throw in an occasional 'yes' or 'really?' and he will regard you as a brilliant conversationalist.

If he should ask for your opinion – which, admittedly, seems unlikely – it is advisable to echo his own. Stick to generalizations and you are unlikely to go wrong. Here are some safe topics:

The evils of communism
The irresponsibility of newspapers and television
The follies of students
The failure of governments to understand business
The importance of profit
The iniquity of taxation
The value of loyalty
The bloodymindedness of trade unions

If you embark on a conversation with his wife, be careful not to make her feel that you consider yourself to be her intellectual superior by talking knowledgeably about books, paintings and wine. Whatever you may think of her, it is essential to preserve a gracious façade. Flattery is usually effective ('What a lovely dress!') but don't overdo it.

She will probably choose one of the following topics:

Her children: Wives of all ages seem to have an extraordinary capacity for deluding themselves that everyone is fascinated by their kids. You will naturally want to talk about your own, but it pays to listen.

The weather: Always a safe subject, especially in countries like Britain.

The servants: If you don't have any servants, throw in a few disparaging comments about garbage collectors, newspaper delivery boys, etc. It will show her that you are on the same side.

Her travels: Most people like to boast about the smart and/or exotic places they have been to. Let her, even if you have been there yourself. If she shows you pictures of her second home in Florida or the South of France, say how envious you are. It will please her enormously.

Her work for charities, clubs, societies. She is probably on two or three committees and will welcome praise for her selfless devotion to the various causes.

THE CORPORATE KID

C hildren, as everyone knows, can be troublesome. Make sure they are not at home when the boss – or a colleague – comes to dinner. If they are in their early teens, they are liable to embarrass you by revealing family secrets. If they are older, they may be going through their socialist phase and, given half a chance, will launch into a vigorous denunciation of capitalism and big corporations. The boss may understand – he probably has rebellious kids of his own – but on the other hand he may not. It is all too easy to jump to the conclusion that an executive who cannot control his own family is unlikely to be able to control his staff.

There is, of course, nothing wrong with being idealistic and one can't blame the young for finding fault with the system. It is, after all, far from perfect. Many adults, too, are concerned about problems like high unemployment and pollution, and disapprove of corporations who do business with countries like South Africa. It is exasperating when your son or daughter starts to talk enthusiastically about Marx and Lenin (while at the same time eagerly accepting whatever financial benefits capitalism has to offer) but parental lectures on the merits of free enterprise are invariably a waste of time. You will simply be regarded as a conformist bore.

Teachers and others who fancy themselves as intellectuals tend to adopt an attitude of moral superiority to the businessman, and their views are bound to influence impressionable young minds. Relax: it probably won't last. Even teachers have a hard time defending what has been happening in countries like Poland, and the chances are that the little horror will change once he or she has to earn a living. At least one big US corporation makes a point of recruiting the most belligerent student rebels: they have, it argues, shown that they possess leadership qualities. 'All you have to do,' explains a spokesman, 'is to make sure that they get married early and take on a mortgage, and that the keys to a company car are dangled under their noses.'

Meantime, alas, they can be an awful nuisance and should be kept at bay. Never invite them along to corporate social occasions, and don't encourage them to visit you at the office, because you can't depend on them to keep their mouths shut. The ideal solution would be to pack them off to the Soviet Union for a while, so that they can see the reality behind the slogans, but the Kremlin isn't keen on having a lot of long-haired idealists roaming around the country. A more practical alternative is to let them live on one of those awful Californian communes for a year or two. It should cure them of their romantic notions.

It is, of course, entirely possible that none of this applies to your kids – that you are blessed with offspring whose sole aim, since nappy days, has been to emulate Daddy and, if possible, to do better. There are precocious children who learn to use a slide rule at seven, invent commercial products at nine, and make a small fortune on the stock market at twelve. 'Computermania' on both sides of the Atlantic has produced a large number of teenage entrepreneurs. In New York, for example, three schoolboys teamed up in 1981 to form a company called Software Innovations. They persuaded their families to invest $1,500 and sold teachers and schoolmates forty shares of stock at $5 each. With the money, they published a catalogue of fifty programs and mailed it to four thousand computer hobbyists. The venture was an instant success. Some of these whiz-kids will no doubt go on to build up sizeable corporations of their own; others will be snapped up by the big organizations and turned into loyal corporation men.

EDUCATING THE CORPORATE KID

Many parents still choose schools or colleges primarily because they are experts at turning children into snobs. Practical considerations take second place. Mummy cannot bear the thought that her darling might have to dirty his hands by doing something useful, like plumbing. It doesn't matter that plumbers nowadays earn more money than teachers or civil servants; he cannot *possibly* become one of them. What would the neighbours say?

The neighbours would probably be delighted that, at last, they have someone among them who knows all about drains. But it is hard to persuade suburban snobs that a blue collar is as good as a white one. So he is sent to a school where they will polish his accent, teach him a little history and Latin, and support the parental contempt for jobs which are associated with the working

"Amco Toy Products were in demand. . ."

classes. What they will *not* teach him is how to hack his way through the business jungle. On the contrary, they may imbue him with all kinds of notions which will turn out to be a serious handicap: ambition is vulgar; money isn't everything; business is tedious; and 'it matters not who won or lost, but how you played the game'.

If he is bright enough to get into a university, he will almost certainly concentrate on the arts. It will probably be a waste of time. A history degree is useless in the business world (unless one has made a point of studying Machiavelli) and an extensive knowledge of literature is more likely to turn him into a dreamer than into a successful executive. A science or engineering degree is more valuable. Easily the best course, though, is to encourage your child – male or female – to take up law or accountancy. At the moment these are the professions which are really making headway in the big corporations.

In Japan, many university graduates nowadays work on production lines. They no doubt hoped to do better, but they have learned to accept that a degree merely shows that one is reasonably intelligent. Academic qualifications are helpful, but they do not *guarantee* success. Many academically brilliant young men and women fail in business; many school drop-outs end up making millions. So there is no need to despair if your offspring doesn't do well at school or university. Soichiro Honda went to a technical high school but got such poor marks that he was asked to leave; he went on to found the world-famous company that bears his name. In America, Jeno Paulucci, a college dropout who built up a large food distribution business, applied for a job in his company under an assumed name. He was rejected as 'unfit for a responsible position' and soon afterwards sold the business for $60 million. Numerous other corporations are headed by men who have had only a very basic education.

Girls still have to work harder than boys if they want a career in business, and the right parental attitude is all-important. You *know* that it's going to be tough, but don't try to dissuade her. Don't assume that she will give up, after a few years, to become a corporate wife and breed children of her own. If a grocer's daughter can become Prime Minister of a country like Britain, there is no reason why your daughter cannot become chief executive of a big corporation.

A brief warning, though, about nepotism. It is not as important a factor as it used to be, chiefly because there are fewer large family-controlled firms, but many people still try to give their children – and relatives – a head start by using whatever influence they have to get them good jobs. If you are tempted, choose another corporation. Nepotism in the business one works for is invariably resented and is likely to do the corporate infighter considerable harm, especially if it turns out that your offspring or son-in-law is not really up to it. Word will quickly reach the top. Even the boss's kids will face a good deal of hostility if they advance too quickly through the ranks.

Baiting the trap

Corporate kids are not impressed by pompous lectures; it is far more effective to stress what they stand to gain by embarking on a business career. Here is a brief list of what is likely to turn them on – and off.

Turn-ons
Jobs in advertising, marketing, public relations, journalism, entertainment, computer programming, banking
Generous salaries
Expense accounts
Company cars
Attractive offices
Long holidays
Big financial deals
Desk computers
Foreign travel
Profit sharing

Turn-offs
Jobs on the production line, book-keeping, anything involving hard work but no glamour
Having to start at the bottom
Pep talks which begin with 'when I was your age . . .'
Having to call everyone 'sir'
Filing
Overtime
Apprenticeship
Commuting
Emphasis on pension schemes
Discipline

HOLIDAYS

John doesn't believe in taking holidays. He knows that the chief executive regards them as a waste of valuable time – he never has a holiday himself – and that a prolonged absence from the office can have unfortunate consequences.

The brass may discover how easily they can do without him and abolish his job while he is away. Or someone else may be sitting at his desk when he gets back.

John encourages his superior to spend three weeks in the South of France during the summer, so that he can step into his shoes and demonstrate that he is not only more dedicated to his work but also more competent. It is a ploy which has proved effective in the past: two years ago he took over from the head of the department he worked for and made the most of several opportunities to impress the chief executive. When the head of the department returned bronzed and relaxed, he was forced into early retirement and John was appointed in his place.

Anne misses the sun, so he sends the family off without him once a year. It leaves him free to spend the evenings at the office and to play golf at weekends. Anne doesn't like this arrangement, but he has managed to persuade her that his career advancement depends on it.

John usually takes a week off during the winter, but explains that he needs time to write reports and strategy papers and takes all the important files with him. He is on the telephone three or four times a day to make sure that his rivals do not exploit the situation.

Last year, John represented the corporation at a convention in Florida and made the pleasant discovery that no one really bothered with the working sessions. Copies of the speeches were distributed in advance and most of the delegates spent the days around the swimming pool, or in the bar, or on the golf course. When he got back, he produced a detailed report and sent a copy to the chief executive. His colleagues were very upset when they heard that he was praised for his efforts. He is trying to get assigned to the next convention in Nice.

The chairman makes regular inspection tours of overseas subsidiaries at appropriate times of the year: Australia in January, France in June, Canada in September and so on. Everyone knows that these are really holidays, at the company's expense, but no one has the courage to say so. Sometimes, the chairman takes an executive along with him. John used to be terribly envious of such people – how marvellous to be given an opportunity to become friendly with the man at the top! – but the recent experience of a rival infighter has taught him that it can be a mixed blessing. The poor man was invited to join the chairman in an evening drinking bout and, unable to hold his liquor, had revealed what they were saying about him at the office. The next morning a sober but furious chairman ordered him to take the next flight home.

Sometimes the corporation *insists* that people take a holiday and even offers to pay for it. This is generally said to be a reward for years of loyal service, but John knows that the aim is to get them out of the way for a while so that they can't oppose controversial decisions or to give the chief executive time to reorganize their departments. Everyone in the corporation knows the story of

"He's a glutton for work – that's as close as he ever gets to a holiday."

the marketing director who was sent on a trip around the world. When he returned he found that (a) someone else had taken his place, (b) the chief executive seemed to have forgotten all about him and was clearly embarrassed by his re-appearance. 'Why don't you,' he suggested, 'go on a trip around the world?' The astonished marketing director pointed out that he had already done just that. 'Well,' said the harassed boss, 'go round again!'

HOBBIES

John has a secret: he belongs to an amateur dramatic society. He doesn't talk about it at the office because he knows that his superiors see it as a sign of weakness – it's almost as bad as confessing that one is interested in ballet. A man who feels the need to be someone else on an amateur stage does not deserve to play a starring role in the corporate theatre.

The basic corporate view of hobbies is that they are a distraction: an ambitious executive should not need any outside activities. Work should also be his hobby: his spare time should be devoted to reading memos, reports, balance sheets and the *Financial Times* or the *Wall Street Journal*.

Most corporations will accept an interest in the *right* kind of sport, such as golf, providing one is willing to make one's skills available when the occasion requires it. From time to time, for example, an executive may be needed to play 'customer golf' – a round or two with an important customer who will, of course, expect to win. Some corporations also have their own teams and a good player can enhance his standing *providing* he isn't foolish enough to beat the chairman or chief executive. By and large, though, enthusiasm for a hobby is regarded as proof that one has divided loyalties, which makes one suspect.

Amateur actors, stamp collectors and Sunday painters are widely thought to be too 'soft' to hold high corporate office. Cycling and soccer are considered working-class pursuits. Writing (especially novel writing) suggests that one is either a dreamer or a rebel. Gardening is for retired people and indicates lack of ambition. If you *must* have a hobby, it is best to stick to one which will strengthen your image as a tough-minded executive.

Some corporations encourage senior employees to take an interest in politics (they like to see their views represented at the national and local level), but, in general, amateur politicians are viewed as potential troublemakers who may take it upon themselves to challenge the system. Any involvement in left-wing organizations is, needless to say, the kiss of death.

Acceptable hobbies

(if you must have one)

Flying
Golf
Rugby
Tennis
Computers
Rowing
Shooting
Sailing
Deep-sea fishing
Polo
Skiing

Suspect hobbies

Stamp collecting
Ballet
Acting
Soccer
Cycling
Gardening
Writing
Left-wing politics
Painting
Scouting

HAVE YOU GOT WHAT IT TAKES?

Test your ability to win the office war (or at least to survive) by answering this simple quiz. There is a grading scale on page 144.

1 You attend yet another meeting and are asked for your views on some hare-brained scheme. Would you:
a) Dismiss it at once?
b) Suggest that the others speak first?
c) Try to find out whose idea it was?
d) Propose that the company conducts some market research?

2 Your employers are taken over by another company and an arrogant newcomer tells you how to do your job. Would you:
a) Protest that you have coped well enough in the past and don't need his advice?
b) Tell him that you are always willing to try new tricks?
c) Threaten to complain to the chief executive?
d) Invite him out for a drink to talk about it?

3 You are told that the marketing director has come up with a great new idea, but you know from experience that it won't work. Would you:
a) Send him a memo pointing out the snags?
b) Suggest that a colleague is better qualified to tackle this important task?
c) Eagerly accept the challenge?
d) Say that you are already deeply involved in another exciting project?

4 The chief executive announces a major cost-cutting campaign. Would you:
a) Insist that you cannot possibly make cuts without jeopardizing the future?
b) Send him a fawning memo, pointing out areas where savings can be made?
c) Lie low until the panic is over and then go on as before?
d) Sack one or more of the troops, and cancel that order for a new office desk?

5 The boss and his wife visit your home for dinner. Would you:
a) Lay on caviar and champagne?
b) Hide the cuckoo clock?
c) Show them your home computer?
d) Proudly introduce them to your teenage children?

6 A colleague suggests that you go off to the nearest bar after work to have 'one for the road'. Would you:

"I'm sorry, Billington, you just don't seem to fit."

a) Refuse?
b) Welcome the chance to discuss your views on office politics with a friend?
c) Go, and order a Virgin Mary?
d) Let him do the talking?

7 You have secured a lucrative contract and would naturally like others to hear about it. Would you:
a) Leave it to your immediate superior to tell the brass?
b) Plant a story in the company journal?
c) Write a memo to the chief executive, telling him the good news?
d) Let an ally do it?

8 You are asked to speak at a company function. Would you:
a) Tell amusing stories about the chief executives?
b) Seize the opportunity to list your achievements?
c) Talk about the exciting opportunities in your field?

d) Make extensive use of slides?

9 A rival uses a lot of fancy jargon at a meeting. Would you:
a) Demand to know what the hell he is talking about?
b) Pretend to understand it?
c) Use some fancy jargon of your own?
d) Stay silent, and let him get away with it?

10 You have decided to ask for more money. Would you:
a) Say that you need more because you find it hard to make ends meet?
b) Try to find out what your colleagues are getting and appeal to the boss's sense of fairness?
c) Point out the current market rate?
d) Threaten to leave if the answer is 'no'?

11 You discover that a rival has made a serious mistake. Would you:

a) Stay out of it?
b) Send him a memo (and a silent copy to the boss) expressing sympathy and offering your help?
c) Report it at once to your superior?
d) Persuade someone else to report it?

12 You are asked to spend a couple of years in the company's office on a delightful Caribbean island. Would you:
a) Accept with alacrity?
b) Suggest that someone else would do a better job?

c) Say that your children's education would suffer?
d) Try to persuade your employers that you are of more use at head office?

13 You hear that your superior is leaving the company. Would you:
a) Wish him good luck, and hope that they'll find a congenial successor?
b) Persuade him to recommend that *you* should succeed him?
c) Find out why he is leaving before making your pitch?
d) Put your case directly to the brass?

"You're free Thursday from lunchtime until the sales meeting at three. We could slot your nervous breakdown into that period."

14 You are offered promotion to a high-risk job. Would you:
a) Eagerly agree to have a go?
b) Ask for time to think about it, and try to discover what you would be letting yourself in for?
c) Say that you'd rather stay where you are?
d) Accept, but insist on a new service contract?

15 You are interviewed by the company newspaper. Would you:
a) Modestly point out that any success you have had is due to the efforts of others?
b) Tell the interviewer how much you enjoy working for this great corporation?
c) Give him your photograph and work in as many plugs as you can?
d) Go out of your way to praise the boss?

"A bit theatrical perhaps, but it's quite dramatic when he bursts through."

"Two hundred and twenty seven copies and step on it!"

Now get your calculator and total up your score

	a)	b)	c)	d)
1	a) 1	b) 3	c) 4	d) 4
2	a) 0	b) 4	c) 0	d) 3
3	a) 1	b) 2	c) 2	d) 3
4	a) 0	b) 4	c) 2	d) 3
5	a) 0	b) 3	c) 3	d) 0
6	a) 2	b) 1	c) 3	d) 3
7	a) 1	b) 2	c) 2	d) 4
8	a) 1	b) 2	c) 4	d) 3
9	a) 2	b) 3	c) 4	d) 1
10	a) 0	b) 3	c) 3	d) 1
11	a) 1	b) 4	c) 1	d) 4
12	a) 0	b) 2	c) 0	d) 4
13	a) 1	b) 3	c) 4	d) 4
14	a) 2	b) 4	c) 1	d) 4
15	a) 1	b) 3	c) 3	d) 4

Evaluating Your Score

If you scored between 91 and 120	You either cheated by looking up the score in advance or you have what it takes to succeed. There is no reason why you should not reach the top.
Between 71 and 90	Not bad. Read this book again and see where you went wrong.
Between 45 and 70	Well, winning isn't everything. You are probably a very nice person, but *do* try to protect yourself against the high scorers.
Between 10 and 44	Forget it. You are not cut out to be a corporate infighter. Lie low and hope for the best.